BEFORE YOU BUY A VINTAGE CAMPER

Copyright © 2021 by CRYSTAL McCULLOUGH

All rights reserved. No part of this book may be reproduced in any manner whatsoever without written permission except in the case of brief quotations embodied in critical articles and reviews.

First Printing, 2021

BEFORE YOU BUY A VINTAGE CAMPER

finding, choosing, assessing, buying, & figuring out what to do with an old camper

CRYSTAL McCULLOUGH

tin & rivet

CONTENTS

NOTE FROM THE AUTHOR vii
DEDICATION ix
ACKNOWLEDGEMENTS xi

1 | INTRODUCTION 1

2 | OLD, CLASSIC, & VINTAGE CAMPERS 15

3 | DECIDING WHAT YOU WANT & NEED 25

4 | BECOMING AN ACTIVE BUYER 35

5 | FINDING OLD CAMPERS FOR SALE 51

6 | HOW MUCH IS THIS OLD CAMPER WORTH? 59

7 | CAMPER UNICORNS 73

8 | KICKING THE TIRES 79

9 | GETTING HOME SAFELY & LEGALLY 99

CONTENTS

10 | **MAKING CHANGES** 109

11 | **LIPSTICK, SCAMS, & POLISHED TURDS** 119

12 | **PARTS, TOOLS, & OTHER COSTS** 129

13 | **MAKING MISTAKES** 139

14 | **RESOURCES** 149

        GLOSSARY 159
      AUTHOR'S STORY 165
   ERRATA, ET CETERA 171

NOTE FROM THE AUTHOR

Dear Readers,

I'm writing this toward the end of 2020, during a time that COVID 19 cases and deaths are growing exponentially even in our small state of Vermont. During this pandemic, old travel trailer prices have risen just as new camper prices have. Scams are rampant, so it's especially important to be careful out there. Parts can be difficult to get since supply chains have been affected by the virus. In the meantime, please stay safe, wash your hands, and wear a mask—including when you check out a camper for sale. I hope to see you on the road or at a rally sooner rather than later.

—CRYSTAL MCCULLOUGH

NOTE FROM THE AUTHOR

DEDICATION

For Jack, Lesley, and Jason.

DEDICATION

ACKNOWLEDGEMENTS

SO MANY PEOPLE HAVE HELPED ME along the way through my old-camper-with-an-old-camper phase. First, thank you to my husband Dwayne who, besides being the love of my life, has let me borrow tools, helped with heavy stuff, and graciously accepted up to five (or was it six?) old campers at a time on our lawn. This is significant because he loves our lawn much more than he loves old campers. And thank you, honey, for talking me down when I wanted to set my camper on fire.

Thank you to Lois and Russell for joining me in Argosy adventures, and to Lois for helping to edit this book. Thank you to Jennie for helping to get some much-needed Zola and Zack stuff done—I plan to put you to work again! Thank you to Lowell for a beautiful countertop for the Mobile Traveler. The new owner loved it. Thank you to Matt for helping Dwayne with the heavier stuff. Thank you to Jess who shares my love of old campers and let me help her work on her Shasta. Thank you to Samara for being my soul sister. Thank you to Lynda for her benevolence. Thank you to Diane for giving the 'ugly blue camper' a new life. Thank you to TR for axle installation and machining custom hinge-shims for me. Thank you to Bob for the welds and sarcasm. Thank you to Eddie for stories of Dad's bus. Thank you to Paula for getting it. Thank you to Brenda for listening.

And thank you to the honest sellers—your integrity keeps this hobby/sideline a happy one.

—CRYSTAL

ACKNOWLEDGEMENTS

More to thank

Many thanks to the old-camper appreciators, owners, renovators, and restorers that share their experience, photos, and videos with those of us who want to learn what they know:

FACEBOOK GROUPS	YOUTUBE CHANNELS
Airstream Argosy Owners	Miller Garage TV
Airstream Restoration	Mortons on the Move
Tin Can Tourists	Mobiletec
Airstream Addicts	Long Long Honeymoon
Vintage Camper Lovers	Drivin' and Vibin'
Vintage Camper Trailers	Flyte Camp
Vintage Campers and Glampers	**CAMPER PROS**
Stone Coat Countertop's Insiders	Justin Taylor, ESK Productions
Airstream Hunter	Jim Roy, Silver Moose Restorations
Vintage Camper Trailers and RVS For Sale	Tim Heintz, Heintz Designs
ONLINE FORUMS	Brian Boone's Got Solar?
Air Forums	Jeff Oliver, Highland Expedition Outfitters
Vintage Trailer Talk	Vintage Trailer Supply

1

INTRODUCTION

WELCOME TO THE BOOK I SHOULD HAVE READ before I ever considered buying an old camper. Honestly, I don't know if I would have gone through with it if I'd known what was ahead on this path of obsession, love, stubbornness, persistence, thrills, mishaps, and lessons. I was correct in my prediction that I would love being an owner, but after that... well, let's just say that there were some surprises. In hindsight, it's clear it would have been more efficient, more cost effective,

I've lost track of how many for-sale travel trailers I've looked at for myself and others. Every single one, no matter how good they look, should be inspected carefully.

and less of an emotional roller coaster to have been armed with even a handful of guidance, insight, and knowledge, which is one of the inspirations behind this book. Overall, I have no doubt that it has been worth it for me. One of the key things we'll be trying to figure out with this book is what defines 'worth it' for you.

Owning a classic or vintage camper is easy enough for anyone: just go buy one. A lot of people do, and are perfectly happy with the simplicity of that option. Other people get burned, broke, and/or overwhelmed, like I did here and there. Like many, I was enamored with the charm, uniqueness, and beauty of vintage and classic campers when starting out. I was missing the whole what-to-look-for and what-to-watch-out-for litany of variables that might have made the subsequent experiences go a little more smoothly. By showing you some of what I faced before, during, and after purchase, I hope to give you insight beyond the charming, unique, and beautiful parts.

Before You Buy a Vintage Camper does not include instructions on how to fix or repair campers, for good reason. There are resources abound that already do this much better than I could. There are no instructions in here on how to decorate, glamp up, or accessorize your camper; again, there are many resources that delve into this already, both in books and online. I share some of my renovation stories in order to show you things I couldn't otherwise, to give you perspective on what can go into these projects, and why you have to consider certain things before buying. Even if you are looking at a completely renovated travel trailer and not planning on getting a fixer-upper, I hope you'll use some of the tips included on what and how to inspect and ask before purchase.

Why I DIY

I went into my first old camper search with the intent to do as much fixing as I could myself, thinking I would save lots of money in doing so. I've since learned that saving money over buying new or already renovated is possible, but it can't be the only motivation. Costs can quickly exceed what was planned, and is one of the reasons my projects can take up to a couple of years to complete. I like the process and learning systems even if at times it seems to take forever to figure out, and then another forever to get it done. Even though this isn't a book about fixing up your old camper by yourself, I'm hoping it might help you realize just how much work goes into getting of these cool things into shape, and whether or not you want to jump in yourself, hire it out, or skip the whole adventure entirely.

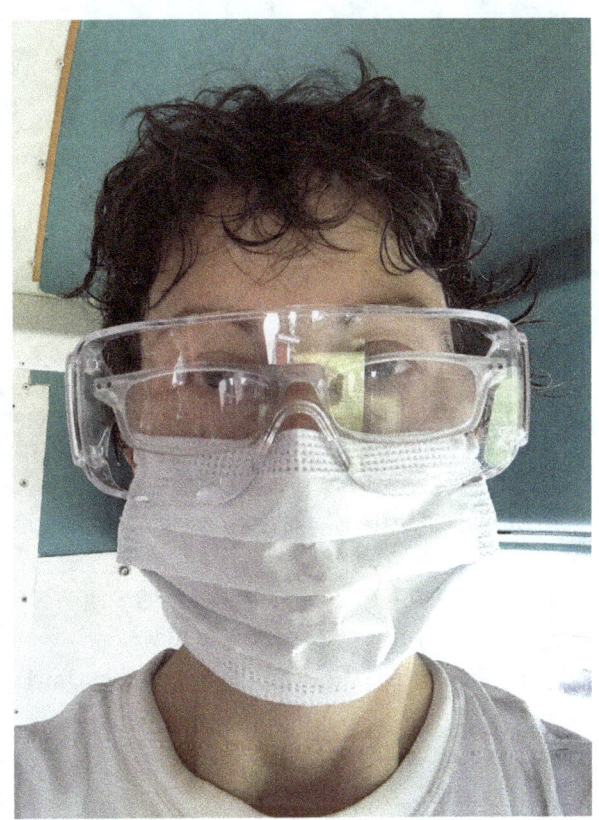

The glamorous life of camper demo.

Not everyone who undertakes the care and feeding of an old camper loves doing it. Not everyone wants to learn what it takes, nor do they want to do what it takes even if they know what it is. I mean really—who wants to spend their time finding leaks that are difficult to track or wait months to get a new axle? Isn't it easier to throw on some paint and to light scented candles in

Doing it yourself takes a lot of work, equipment, tools, room, good weather, and gumption. And soap. And rivets.

a camper instead of seeking out and removing rot and mold? If we're going to have to spend a bunch of money, why not get something new?

Thankfully, for those who want to skip doing the work themselves, there are trusty, experienced restorers and renovators around the U.S. Spend some time in any online forum and you will hear stories about wonderful, talented experts. Sadly, you'll also hear about so-called professionals that rip people off.

As much as some people want to delve deep into a camper project, there are others who prefer to buy a vintage or classic camper that has already been totally renovated and/or updated and ready to hit the road. There are still others who have a plan and the means to hire a professional restorer/renovator to repair and rebuild a travel trailer to their specifications. This book is for those of you

You can't predict everything you'll want in a travel trailer, but it's beneficial to think about it prior to buying. It's becoming increasingly desirable and affordable to add solar panels to travel trailers, especially if you plan to travel off the grid. Your roof will need enough room to mount panels if that's where you want them to be, and you'll have to add a solar controller to control the amount of charge going to your battery. You can do this yourself or hire a pro to do it for you. (AS)

who match this description, too, since you'll still have to assess the quality of a camper, figure out if the price you're paying is fair, and decide what you want and need in a rebuild or refurbish. It's perfectly fine to be the designer of your new-to-you camper and to hire out work to professionals. And just as fine to buy one already completely fixed up. I am one of the people who embrace the experience and want—maybe even need—to take on the part of the journey that involves all the steps after a camper is purchased. Plus, I couldn't afford new or to hire someone to help me, so I had to embrace it or let projects rust and rot in the backyard. What fun would that be?

There are some painful and tedious parts to doing renovation work, like removing and labeling panels and the cleaning walls (look at that grunge!). Organization and keeping track of parts is a necessary part of the process.

The renovation process has its painful and frustrating moments (and days, and weeks, and months), but has been more rewarding than I could have imagined. In my 1972 Airstream Argosy 20 I've had to take apart things I've thought were finished and start over. There are times I have to ask for help—and if you're anything like me, no matter how much proof I have that asking for help is a good thing, I can stubbornly and defiantly refuse to ask for it as long as I can. There is a constant challenge of problem solving that I love 95 to 97 percent of the time. I've logged some hours of tears and some staring blankly at a camper with my hands on my hips. I count both of these activities as critical parts of the process.

Parts of my renovation projects are tedious and boring—like removing old screws and staples and cleaning aluminum wall panels. But I'm giddy when I figure out how something works—even simple things like flipping a switch and having a light go on.

Because I decided to take on the work myself, my skill set has grown to include basic 12v and 110 wiring, plumbing, metal work, buck riveting, lighting, insulation installation, and painting. As an unintended bonus, the process of tearing down and renovating campers has paralleled some tearing down and renovating of myself. I had no idea this would happen, so it's easy to say that I've exceeded expectations.

I read an article in *The New York Times* about the American chef Samin Nosrat and her love of gardening. This is what struck me the most: "Gardening makes Samin Nosrat happier. Yanking out weeds, composting for hours at a time and planting seeds have become a kind of solace, 'regenerating both the soil and something deep in myself,' she writes."

My campers are to me what Chef Nosrat's garden is to her. Working on campers gave me permission to look inside the walls, to acknowledge and tear out the rot and ruin, and forced me to work hard to build it back up. I had to ask for help, and to do things I'd never done before all by myself. I made some major mistakes and missteps, and have had to force myself to accept and amend the areas that I messed up. The steps I've taken have been a tangible analogy of life for me, and forces me to focus on what was right in front of me. I embrace and appreciate the experience, although admittedly, embracing and appreciating can take a significantly longer amount of time and effort when something goes wrong or not as expected.

No matter which direction you take, one of these beautiful bundles of aluminum, steel, wood, and rubber will likely change your life.

Who are Zola and Zack and why do I write about them?

Throughout the book, I refer to Zola and Zack, my two classic Airstream Argosys. The names came about when I realized Zola looked like a big Zoloft pill. When I got the 28-foot Argosy, I stayed with the chill-pill theme and named it Zack, after Prozac. I've owned and sold several other brands/models of old campers, but these are two that I've intended to be mine since I got them.

Zola and Zack are my two 1970s Airstream Argosys.

In case you were wondering, a lot of people name their campers, and there are no rules about it. Like boats, they often are what would traditionally be considered female names and referred to as *her*, and there are also some hims and gender-neutrals. Before I got them, Zola's name was *The Twinkie* and Zack's name was *Gus*. My husband Dwayne calls them *your small camper* and *your big camper*.

Since Zola and Zack have been my biggest and most personal projects, they are often part of my story and you'll hear their names throughout this book. They both have given me an awful lot to write about for you.

Me enjoying one of the many facets of camper ownership.

A little about me

In my day job, I'm an author and editor, and have written several how-to books in the consumer computer industry and one in the running-race industry—both areas in which I was largely self-taught. I lean toward being autodidactic when I'm fascinated with something, and campers have been no exception.

I know a lot more than I used to, but I am not a camper expert and won't try to convince you that I am. I am driven to write and teach about what I've learned to hopefully help you skip—or at least, not be surprised by—some of the more awkward parts of the overall process. I'll give you a glance into what I faced when I made the decision to get a camper in case you're curious what you'll be up against.

Besides renting campers, going to a camper rally open house is a great opportunity to see and learn about old campers. This is a 1951 Roadmaster I saw at the Pismo Vintage Trailer Rally.

Using a camper taught me as much as when fixing her up. Which brings me to one of my favorite tips: If you're not sure if you're going to like this vintage camper stuff, rent one and take it on a trip, or spend a weekend at a campsite that has vintage rentals there for you to stay in. Check some suggestions in the Resources chapter.

Once you make the decision to move forward, I hope that my story will help to empower you through your progression into vintage, classic, and old camper ownership.

I've had a *lot* of fun, a ton of feeling-accomplished, and have done some good work that I'm proud of. I've met some incredible people along the way, both in person and virtually—that have

One mistake I made was to use the wrong primer for the galvanized steel endcaps on my Argosy. Bad prep = bad paint. It had to be redone.

helped me and/or I've helped them. Any regrets are primarily due to miscalculations and plain ol' mistakes. Mistakes I made along the way have made me more attentive to details—not that I wasn't interested in details before, but now I get why we're supposed to pay attention to them. Some mistakes were naive and purely by accident—maybe I misunderstood what needed to be done or didn't have instructions, or followed instructions but not far enough, like sealing something but not using enough caulk because I thought it would look too messy. Others were often the result of impatience—I just wanted to be done and to get out camping. I mean, what are the chances of all those camper experts being right, right? :-/ Answer: A lot more of a chance than me. One of my biggest and most expensive mistakes was due to skipping one step because I thought I didn't need to do it. You'll read about that in the Making Mistakes chapter.

Not everyone is bias, but everyone else is

Here's a discussion I had recently:

I hear a knock at the door, I answer. There's a man standing there.

"I stopped because I saw the campers out here," he said, "Is the boss at home?"

"I'm the boss," I said. He laughed.

"No, I meant can I talk to the guy who did all the work on the campers?"

"I'm the guy," I said.

Even if my husband tells anyone who asks about them that the campers are my projects and not his, they will often default to looking at and talking to him until he's said *you have to ask her* enough times, or he walks away. In this case, the person seemed pleasantly surprised that I was the boss and 'the guy', and he we went on to have a great discussion about my campers.

Art by Angelina Bambina, licensed via Adobe Stock.

As a 50-something woman, I've experienced this kind of interchange for a long time, and some haven't been that pleasant. I started my professional editorial/writer career in my 20s at a national personal-computer magazine. Going to technology trade shows in those days meant that I was one of the very few women on the show floor that was not a model (then referred to as "booth babes") or a marketing rep in a tradeshow booth. If I walked around with one of the male editors, many people would address him and not me, even though I was the one asking questions and had a very visible press badge hanging around my neck.

A couple of years ago, Dwayne and I went to a truck-cap retailer to buy a cap for his pickup. Dwayne was deciding about the kind of windows he wanted in the cap when the salesperson motioned toward me and said to him, "You'll want more windows if she ever drives your truck. Women don't know how to use mirrors to back up."

I turned to Dwayne (he knew what was coming next; he's known me for a while) and said in my best deadpan voice, "Yes, honey, that's right. I forgot that women don't know how to use mirrors." Then I walked away, because I've also known myself for a while. Dwayne told me the salesperson

$$\sum F = ma \quad f = \frac{1}{T} \quad \oint E \cdot ds = -\frac{\partial}{\partial t} \quad \sum F = ma \quad f = \frac{1}{T} \quad \oint E \cdot ds = -\frac{\partial}{\partial t}$$

$$H = QD \quad t' = \frac{t}{\sqrt{1-v^2/c^2}} \quad H = QD \quad t' = \frac{t}{\sqrt{1-v^2}}$$

$$\psi(r,t) + V(r)\psi(r,t) \quad p = mv \quad E = hf \quad \psi(r,t) + V(r)\psi(r,t) \quad p = mv \quad E = hf$$

$$\tau = rF\sin\theta \quad i\hbar\frac{\partial}{\partial t}\psi(r,t) = -\frac{\hbar^2}{2m}\nabla^2\psi(r,t) + V(r)\psi(r,t) \quad \tau = rF\sin\theta \quad i\hbar\frac{\partial}{\partial t}\psi(r,t) = -\frac{\hbar^2}{2m}\nabla^2$$

$$\Delta x \geq \frac{\hbar}{2} \quad \bar{\omega} = \frac{\Delta\theta}{\Delta t} \quad \sin\theta_c = \frac{n_2}{n_1} \quad \Delta p_x \Delta x \geq \frac{\hbar}{2} \quad \bar{\omega} = \frac{\Delta\theta}{\Delta t} \quad \sin\theta_c = \frac{n_2}{n_1} \quad \Delta p_x$$

$$f_{low} \quad \sum F = \frac{dp}{dt} \quad f_{beat} = f_{high} - f_{low} \quad \sum F = \frac{dp}{dt} \quad f_{beat} = f_{high}$$

$$f = \frac{1}{T} \quad \oint E \cdot ds = -\frac{\partial \Phi_B}{\partial t} \quad f = \frac{1}{T} \quad \oint E \cdot ds = -\frac{\partial \Phi_B}{\partial t} \quad t' = \frac{t}{\sqrt{1-v^2}}$$

$$E = mc^2 \quad \sum F = ma \quad t' = \frac{t}{\sqrt{1-v^2/c^2}} \quad E = mc^2 \quad \sum F = ma$$

$$v = v_0 + at \quad v = v_0 + at$$

$$F_g = -\frac{Gm_1m_2}{r^2}\hat{r} \quad \bar{\omega} = \frac{\Delta\theta}{\Delta t} \quad p = mv \quad F_g = -\frac{Gm_1m_2}{r^2}\hat{r} \quad \bar{\omega} = \frac{\Delta\theta}{\Delta t} \quad p = mv$$

$$L = mrv\sin\theta \quad L = mrv$$

$$f_{beat} = f_{high} - f_{low} \quad \sum F = \frac{dp}{dt} \quad f_{beat} = f_{high} - f_{low} \quad \sum F = \frac{dp}{dt}$$

$$\frac{\partial \Phi_B}{\partial t} \quad \frac{\partial \Phi_B}{\partial t}$$

How to back up a travel trailer.
Image by amovitania, licensed via Adobe Stock.

was mystified, asked him if I was mad, and why. Later, the salesperson approached me and quietly said that he was sorry and that it was wrong of him to say what he did. So, that's progress.

It's a part of my personality to set the record straight with people who have perceptions or bias about me and anyone/anything else if I can. It's insanely more difficult to release myself from my own preconceptions than others. For example, I will be the first person to tell you that anyone can learn how to back up a trailer successfully. But for the first couple of years, I was pretty sure that I was born with the inherent inability to back up trailers, and knew if I tried that I would flounder about and run into things—both things I didn't want to do. I avoided it by choosing pull-through camping spaces. I watched YouTube videos, bookmarked advice people gave to others. I was confused by suggestions like "steer the opposite way you want to go and then turn your wheels to follow the camper." My biggest enemy was overthinking it, i.e. *Why does everyone else understand the Nonequilibrium Applications of Newton's Laws of Motion and I don't?*

Eventually, I realized that I had to apply the laws of superlotto: *You're not going to win if you don't play*. So, I did what I should have done, and practiced until I could do it. What I wish I had done in hindsight was to allow myself to not feel so inadequate because I thought I couldn't do it. That's left over from a lifetime of not wanting to do something that I didn't already excel at, which kept me from trying a lot of things.

If other people can do it, we can, too—but we also have the choice that we don't have to if we don't want to. It can take longer to learn some things that it might have taken someone else, or it may be way easier than expected. In the case of backing up, there is a reason that nearly every campground has pull-through sites, and it's not because of me—many people prefer the ease of pulling through rather than backing up. What I'm getting at is that for me, learning out of fear is almost always a struggle. I've found my own biases to be much tougher to deal with than others'. I hope you take this all at your own pace, and enjoy it as much as you are able.

Let's get going

I hope this book will save you some time, money, and angst. I hope it will make you smile and even swear a little bit, if that's what it takes. I can't guarantee you a regret-free experience, but I can share what I've learned from successes and mistakes with the hopes that you can avoid the mistakes part. I invite you to share with me what you learn [crystal@tinandrivet.com], so I can keep learning, too.

2

OLD, CLASSIC, & VINTAGE CAMPERS

THERE ARE VARYING OPINIONS on what makes a camper "vintage." Automobiles in collector clubs are usually considered antique if they are over 45 years old, vintage if they were manufactured 25-45 years ago, and classic if they are at least 20 years old. Your state's department of motor vehicles will have its own definition of antique in order to register a car, motorhome, or trailer

In the 80s, U-Haul rented fiberglass campers through its subsidiary Rec Vee. When U-Haul retired Rec Vee, they made the campers available for sale to the public. These would be considered 'classic' travel trailers.

as such. The longest-running camper-membership club in the country, Tin Can Tourists [tincantourists.com], sorts campers into four categories based on the year in which they were made:
- Antique — 1945 and earlier
- Vintage — 1946-1969
- Classic — anything over 20 years old that isn't vintage or antique
- New — anything newer than 20 years old.

Some trailer rallies have their own definition of vintage—Trailerfest Vintage Camper Trailer Rallies, for example, specifies that campers should be made before 1979 to attend its namesake annual event. Others will label all older campers "vintage" in connection with the decade in which they were made, i.e. "vintage 1950s" or "vintage 1980s."

When speaking of generalities in this book, I interchangeably use "old" to define a camper that is more than 20 years old, and needs money, time, skill, and imagination beyond its initial purchase to make it into what you want it to be. Camper historians or purists may roll their eyes at my daring to use words like "old" and "vintage" in the same context this way. Please know that my intent with this book isn't to change the traditional generalities that define any camper group—I'm simply trying to avoid having to say "antique, vintage, classic, and other older campers" each time I make a general statement.

Does it matter? Of course, if it does to you. Arguably any not-new camper, whether it's 6 or 60 years old, will probably need some work done, whether it's as simple as aesthetic updates because you hate the wallpaper or the curtains, to complete rebuilds in order to be road- and camp-worthy.

It stands to reason that if you're reading this book you already have at least a little bit of an inkling of desire to get an old camper and make it yours. If you're one of those people that isn't at all convinced that getting an old camper and fixing it up is on your bucket list, here are some good things I like about old campers that might help you make up your mind:

1. They are often less expensive than new campers (prior to restoration);
2. They were built to be less expendable than newer campers;
3. There's not nearly as much dull brown in them as in new campers;
4. They have character;
5. They have stories;
6. If taken care of properly, they can appreciate in value; and
7. It can be really rewarding to own, successfully renovate, remodel, or restore a camper whether you do it yourself or hire the work out.

To be fair, here are some bad things about old campers:

1. They can smell really bad;

One positive about old campers is that they can be so freekin' cute. It can take a lot of work and money to get them that way.

2. They can have unchecked and hidden water damage;
3. They might not have a clear title (or any title), which is critical in some states in order to register the camper;
4. If the previous owners had animals in there and you have allergies to said animals, you could be sneezing instead of camping;
5. Mold could be lurking anywhere moisture can get to;
6. The cost to fix could shoot well over your budget, whether you do it yourself or hire the work out to pros;

7. You might not have a weather-proof place to park it or work on it, so you may have an additional rental or build cost;
8. It can be difficult (but not impossible) to get insurance;
9. There's no warranty unless you're getting it through a dealer and they choose to offer one;
10. You don't know what's happened in them;
11. You don't want to know what's happened in them;
12. It can be really frustrating and overwhelming to successfully renovate, remodel, or restore a camper yourself, or to trust someone to do it for you;
13. You will make mistakes, and some will be costly or take a lot of time to fix; and
14. Some campgrounds do not allow travel trailers over 10 years old.

You might have noticed that there are twice as many reasons *not* to get an old camper than to get one. If pressed, I could probably come up with a whole lot more reasons not to do it, like *climbing on a curved camper roof can be scary especially when it's raining* and *sometimes you have to tear it apart more than once to get it right*. So—what the hell is wrong with me? What am I doing here writing about these crazy time and money suckers? Why did I obsessively buy more than one old camper even though I thought I'd only be interested in fixing up one? Did I even know why I got this first camper in the first place? Did I realize how many major mistakes I would make?

Why am I doing this?

Things might have been easier and made more sense if I had taken the advice that I am about to give you: Before you buy your new-to-you camper, think about why you're feeling the urge to get one. If you're like me, you're going to have to convince yourself once in a while that what you got yourself into is worth it. In fact, I'd suggest writing down why you wanted a camper so that you don't forget it. Maybe have it framed and hung on the wall of your gutted camper so you can read it every time you work on it.

My niece Jess uses her Shasta Airflyte as a mobile store and workspace, as well as for family camping. Since it's a 1960s model, it's considered vintage.

"What have I gotten myself into?" and "Why am I doing this?" are questions I still ask myself every once in awhile. It can take a lot of time to go over all of the reasons that may have spurred me and many others to buy an old camper.

Some people want a camper because their family has been camping since they can remember. Some have family members that have campers, and that inspires them to get one, too. In my case, a few years ago my brother Tom built a customized class C camper/toy hauler out of a retired mu-

My friend Cindy decided to use her Airstream—formerly owned by her parents—as a full-time home. I hauled it to Arizona from Michigan for her.

nicipal shuttle bus for his business, and I loved it. He said more than once in his trademark laconic way that he would never do it again—which, for some reason, made me want to find a fixer-upper camper and try the same thing even more.

Some people eye campers because they are wanting to camp in something more solid and pre setup than a tent. While tent camping has its own appeal, I prefer to have solid walls around me. And an indoor bathroom. And no rocks under my mattress.

Some are looking for an alternative to a tiny house to live in. That wasn't an idea for me from the get-go, but in the last couple of years, I've grown to like the idea of living on the road as a full- or part-time digital nomad, or being a snowbird and spending winters in my camper somewhere warm.

Some people plan to travel, either on their own or with their family. They might want a home-away-from-home that is more sustainable and has less of a carbon footprint than their 'normal' house or vacation destination. Or maybe the goal is to get off the grid. Way, waaaaay off the grid. How better to do that than with a moving house?

With COVID19 significantly impacting traditional travel, new and used RVs have been selling like hotcakes. These buyers are planning for an alternative vacation and/or to have a bug-out vehicle at hand if a natural or other disaster happens.

Some people have watched episodes of *Flippin' RVs* and thought to themselves that they could also buy a camper for four figures, restore it, and then sell it for five or even six figures. As idealistic as this might be as a whole, there are several people who rescue and renovate and restore campers for a living after they've renovated just one for themselves. Some have very lucrative businesses. Some do not. Just keep in mind that it's not as easy as the 42-minute episode might make it seem. The return on investment is dependent on a lot of variables, especially talent and skill.

Some people want to get a camper to rent and make some extra money. I use Airbnb to rent my small Argosy out on our property, and Outdoorsy to rent it off of our property. There are benefits (meaning: income) to this, and some annoyances (meaning renters that break things and leave messes, etc.).

My friend Kate designed her 1963 Airstream Overlander International Land Yacht to be a mobile classroom and event space called The Atomic Classroom [atomicclassroom.com]. The folks at ESK Productions in Vermont built a stage/bar out of an Argosy [no URL because they have since closed], and Miller Garage in Texas started its renovation business after transforming a 1970s Airstream into a coffee shop [youtube.com/c/MillerGarage]. These are only a few creative alternative spaces made out of campers.

Some people want to use a camper as a home office, guest house, and/or a she/he shed. Others buy old campers to convert into ice fishing shanties (or bob houses). Some want a project and it looks like fun.

In short, I can't convince anyone (but you) that your reason for buying an old camper to fix up is valid. You can buy a camper for whatever reason you want, or for no reason at all. But I *can* strongly

BEFORE YOU BUY A VINTAGE CAMPER

ESK Productions in Vermont built this stage/event space from an Airstream Argosy.

suggest, again, that you write down or memorize your reasons. That list will come in very handy as a mental backup, especially if you find yourself knee deep in wood rot and frame corrosion later on.

An Airstream retrofitted into a food trailer. (AS)

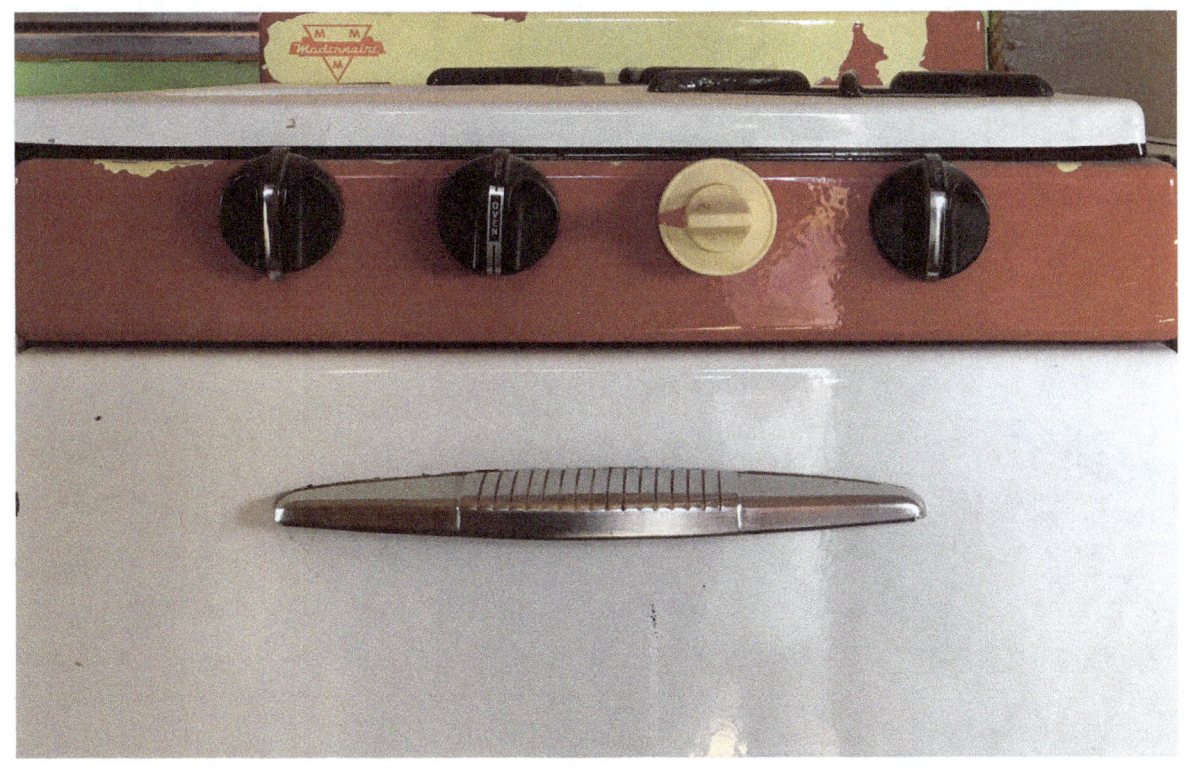

3

DECIDING WHAT YOU WANT & NEED

BEFORE YOU SPEND YOUR HARD-EARNED MONEY, it's helpful to have a general idea of what you're going to want and need for systems and amenities in a camper. You may not be able to predict everything you'll want and need, but knowing at least some can hasten the purchasing process because you can at least weed out the campers you're pretty sure you don't want. It will also help you decide if the project ahead of you is worth the money and work.

I loved this camper, but I really wanted a full-time bed rather than a couch that I would have to convert into a bed every night.

When I was searching for my first camper, I was looking for a safe and cozy space that would be mine, that would have my imprint on it and be a place where I wanted to be. I really wanted an Airstream, and because of my budget I knew it would have to be one that needed a lot of work. I needed a bed, a toilet, and a locking entry door. It only occurs to me right now as I write this that I didn't get those three things (bed, toilet, locking door) with the camper when I bought it; I had to add each one. I wanted to have a camper that had a full-time bed, not one I'd have to make every day out of a table or couch. This generally requires more room in a travel trailer than one that has a multipurpose couch/bed or booth/bed.

I've found that as time has gone by and the more I camp, the more I come up with little things here and there I'd change or do differently. I think that's a pretty normal experience for those of us who are new to this adventure.

Consider toilets and showers. Some people won't ever use a toilet or shower in a camper, while some people demand these as internal provisions. Many old campers, especially small vintage ones, don't have a shower, and may not even have a toilet. Many campgrounds have public bathrooms and showers that guests can use, so if you are comfortable with using their facilities, then you won't miss the missing shower in your camper.

When I first started out seriously seeking a camper to fix up, I felt like it would be cheating if I had amenities like a microwave, a refrigerator, a shower, and a TV in my camper. I mean, camping was supposed to be… you know… *camping*. Roughing it. Going against the norms. Cooking over a fire or propane stove and embracing the dirt and bugs that made their way into the food. I was confused about the huge new campers at campgrounds with their indoor and outdoor televisions, huge refrigerators, air conditioning, and one and a half baths. Didn't they know that's not real camping?

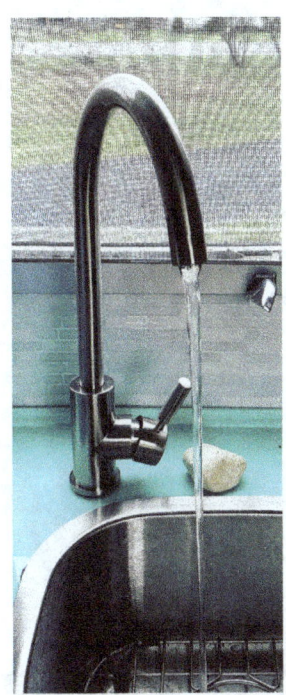

I wanted some basic amenities in my camper, and added all of them. For example, running water was a top priority for me. Some camper owners don't care if they have water and plumbing.

It took one trip to figure out that I liked things that made life a little more non-rough, like running water and coffee that took less than 10 minutes to brew. I was using my camper Zola more to travel than to camp, using her like a hotel room rather than a replacement for a tent. I liked having food that needed to stay cold to stay cold, and after driving all day, throwing something in the microwave for three minutes before collapsing into bed became a necessity.

So, as I continued with Zola's build, a few things changed: I added running water and a teeny microwave. If I'm plugged in, I can microwave my dinner and go to sleep rather than have to set up

A big bathtub would be glorious on a camping trip! But only when hooked up to a water source, since carrying this amount of water in a tank in an average vintage or classic camper is impractical.

my propane stove outside and cooking something from scratch. If I want to "camp-camp" I still can. I like having the flexibility of having that choice.

I knew my must-have list had to be *my* must-have list. If you need a jacuzzi tub and a big-screen TV in your camper, then by all means go for it. Google *Furrion Elysium Luxury RV* for inspiration. You might not need a helipad on your camper, but at least you know that you can if you want to.

Imagination, skill, and budget determined what I would end up with and how long the entire build would take. Over the course of her two-year build, I was able to equip Zola with what I wanted and needed that fit within my budget—although admittedly, I did not have a dollar amount in mind when I started—that's one reason it took two years to finish.

With such a small camper, a fold-away table worked best for me. This one was made with a Lagun table mount so it could be tucked under the aqua-blue shelf when not needed.

There are items I may add or change as time goes along, such as adding propane tanks back and installing an indoor stove and a propane-powered heater. There have only been a couple of nights when I wish I'd put in an air conditioner. It may still happen—and just in case, I had wired it to power one if I changed my mind in the future.

My 28-foot camper has a different list of wants and needs. This bigger camper is being built out specifically as a home-on-wheels—a tiny house made out of a classic camper. I want to be able to boondock (camp without water, sewer, and electrical hookups) and still have amenities such as refrigeration and hot water. The bed has to be easier to make since making the bed in my little Argosy is frustratingly difficult due to being closed in on three sides. The big Argosy will have a standard camper flush toilet rather than a composting toilet, and a gray and black tank.

The big camper also has an upgraded roof air conditioner, unlike the small one, and a built-in heater. If this becomes a snow-bird home that we live in for months at a time, then an RV washer-dryer would be a nice add if we choose not to stay in a campground with a laundry facility.

Its fridge is a lot larger than the one in the small camper, and bigger than its original one. It's a good size for a couple of weeks of groceries for two, and runs on both 12v and 110 household current.

On the next handful of pages, I'm sharing an empty version of a "want" list. When you want to start your own camper quest, rate each item, whether a camper has it originally or you may have to add it. There's space to add your own items if I missed something you want. There's no right or wrong here, it's simply an exercise in figuring out what you might want.

Some may look at this list and consider a few of the items as overkill or overly ambitious. Some are unrealistic—for example, if you have your heart set on a 10-foot Shasta Compact, you won't be able to fulfill your wish for a full-size refrigerator. If you prove me wrong, please send photos.

I encourage you to use your resulting list as a guide to your priorities if you start looking at campers for sale. Along the way, your needs and wants may change, and again, that's OK. You might see a layout that is perfect for you that is nothing like what you had imagined, or find a camper for sale that meets all your top wants and more. You may find that you never use a particular item and decide to remove it to make more storage room.

Or maybe you'll change your mind about an old camper altogether. It's better to know that before you buy. Rank each of the items in the table with these qualifiers.

1 = Yes, I must have!
2 = That would be nice.
3 = Undecided.
4 = Not a deal breaker.
5 = Whatever.

BEFORE YOU BUY A VINTAGE CAMPER

a full-time bed	an electric jack
a camper toilet	dinette booth
a composting toilet	lots of windows
running water	a bunk bed
ceiling fan	all original appliances
air conditioning	high clearance for back roads
an oven	washer/dryer
an inside cooktop	dishwasher
lots of storage	space for kids
space for a dog	space for adult guests
space for a cat (and litter box)	all LED lights
light weight	a secure lock on the door
12v power (off battery)	a bathroom sink
110v power (plug in for power)	a shower
room to stand up	a bathtub
solar panels	a place for a spare tire
new wiring	a skylight
new wheels/tires	a ceiling vent

CRYSTAL MCCULLOUGH

a fridge	a fireplace
a freezer	a wood stove
a spice rack	an awning
a particular brand	a particular brand & model
gray tank	built-in heater
black tank	television
a bed that's easy to make	dog crate

BEFORE YOU BUY A VINTAGE CAMPER

Let's start the search for your camper.

My hotel room in Santa Barbara, CA.

4

BECOMING AN ACTIVE BUYER

I FIRST SAW PHOTOS OF ZOLA, my 1972 Airstream Argosy 20, in a post on Facebook in late 2016. The then-owner posted five photos of her in a private group of Airstream Argosy owners, listed what work he had done, and said he was gauging interest in the sale of his camper because he and his family hadn't used it in a few years. I saved the post, but, for whatever reason, I didn't reach out to him for a while.

Let me back up a bit.

I'd been seriously obsessing over and looking for an older Airstream for over a year and a half after spotting a tiny 1961 Bambi on the side of the road with a handwritten FOR SALE sign on it. Prior to that, I'd been introduced to the whole idea of getting and fixing up an old camper by my sister Diane, who I had followed around at a vintage camper show looking at travel trailers in various stages of restoration and renovation. I was intrigued with the spirit of these old campers. There were tiny Serro Scottys, and huge Spartan Royal Mansions. There were several Shastas and a handful of rarities, like a canned ham Metzendorf from Ohio and a tiny fiberglass Trillium.

And then there were the Airstreams, which were one of the few brands I'd heard of. I loved the curved roof, the retro color schemes, and found out that they had a tremendous history, an almost cult-like following, and were made to last. But that was the extent of my knowledge.

My dad's 'bus house' in progress. It was made from the back ends of two International busses joined together. The photo was taken in the late 1950s or early 1960s.

Campers played small parts in my life before this. Before I was born, my dad had built a huge camping bus from the back of one bus welded to the back of another—making it a very odd-looking entity, but functional for a family of seven. He, my mom, and my five siblings traveled in it, but I only knew the bus as a run-down storage container and as a structure to dive under with my brother Bob when he'd shoot arrows straight up into the air to see where they'd land.

My father has been gone for 35 years, but my older siblings remember a few details about the bus. It was an International with the back of another bus used as the front. It was registered as a "bus house." When you walked in, you had to step up to get into the driving area. There was no driver's-side door. My oldest brother Ed said that our dad stopped working on it because he got seriously ill with galvanize poisoning as a result of welding and torching its galvanized metal.

The little Bambi on the side of the road.

Fast forward back to the road-side Bambi. I had driven by it a half dozen times, and finally called the number on the sign. I asked the seller if my husband and I could take a look. Neither one of us knew what to look for, but his years as a professional carpenter and renovator gave me confidence to be able to assess its fixability fairly well.

I walked in the door and immediately started imagining life with this little camper. I knew that you're not supposed to buy the first one you see, but rules were made to be broken, I told myself. I loved the idea of owning such a classic travel trailer, the price they were asking seemed reasonable compared to others I'd seen for sale online, and it was all original from what I could tell—down to the mattresses, light fixtures, and toilet. On the negative side, though, it had the original mat-

I walked in the door and immediately started imagining life with this little camper.

tresses, light fixtures, and toilet. There was no A/C—not even a fan—and it had very few windows. It smelled musty, and there was water damage near the front windows. There were mouse droppings in the drawers and in the cabinets. The mattresses looked good but stunk.

Now I can look at that Bambi with a little bit of camper experience on my side. I now know that some water damage is fairly normal in some older Airstreams, some of which is fairly simple to fix, and some of which requires a complete overhaul. I know now that nearly any camper that has been sitting will get some mouse visitors, so unless it's a bona fide infestation, it doesn't have to be a deal breaker.

Even without knowing this stuff, I was pretty certain her asking price of $7,000 was a good deal, and I considered buying it even if it was just to flip and make some money toward another Airstream. I had a limited budget, and I wanted to be smart about the purchase. I made a pros and cons list, and finally made the decision that I'd go for it.

When I called the owner to make my offer, she told me that the Bambi had sold earlier that week. I learned a new lesson pretty quickly: desirable campers at good prices sell fast.

In the next few months, the obsession to get an Airstream grew to the point that I think I'd joined nearly every Airstream and vintage camper group on Facebook that exists, subscribed to Airstream Classifieds, and joined AIR Forums—a huge online bulletin board for Airstream owners. Dwayne wasn't all that thrilled about the thought of getting a camper, but he did humor me and go with me to a couple of camper dealerships, including the closest Airstream dealer about two hours away. He patiently walked through all the Airstreams and listened to the salesperson's script. He didn't balk when he saw how much a new Airstream costs (prices range from the "cheap" ones that start around $35,000 up to a very healthy six figures), although he was quick to point out on our trip home that he had no desire to lay out that kind of money on a camper, even on a payment plan. That I already knew, but it was an invaluable experience for me to see the different layouts and features, and I continued to obsess about how to get one of these beautiful things. Like every solid obsession, it felt like life wouldn't be right until I had one. If only I had an Airstream, we could go on weekend camping trips, and he could go fishing and I could... well, sit around in the Airstream!

I continued to look at other brands of old travel trailers, but tried to view every Airstream that was for sale within a couple of hundred miles. I was able to look at several different sizes, models, and ages of Airstreams, all the way up to a huge, triple-axle 1990's Airstream.

I learned about the Argosy line of Airstreams when one came up for sale on a local Craigslist search. I had never heard of the Argosy, but I was intrigued by the painted Airstream and sent the seller a bunch of questions. His photos showed a lot of interior and exterior damage, and it had been parked for a long time in one place. His price point was close to $10,000, and I had no idea if that was a fair price. I tried multiple times to try to go see it in person, but his replies to me were cryptic and somewhat rude—either I was annoying him with all of my naive questions, or he was just not very nice—or both. Eventually, he stopped replying to me.

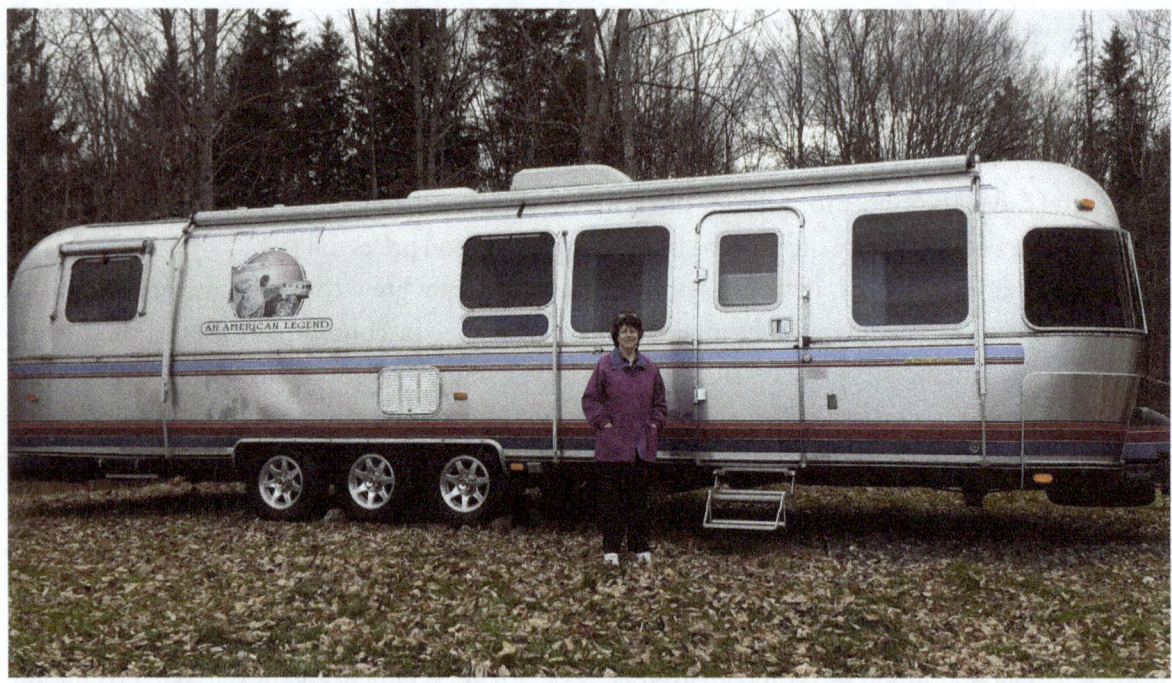

My sister Diane in front of a triple-axle 1997 Limited Edition 34-foot Airstream, one of 50 made to commemorate the work of painter Norman Rockwell. It was in great shape, but it was a little too big for me.

My second buying lesson: There are some camper sellers that will ignore questions and not reply no matter how nice/educated/serious you are about a potential purchase. And I get it—many people want to sell things quickly, not spend time educating everyone on the thing they are selling. Then there are the sellers who include only one or two photos, and then get mad if you ask for more photos. Please know that this isn't personal (unless you're a grumpy person)—you can join any online camper group and you will hear stories of grumpy sellers who seem like they don't really want to sell or who feel the need to let you know that they know more than you do, and can't be bothered with questions or picture-taking.

I gladly missed out on this particular travel trailer and added *Argosy* to the list campers to look for. I joined the Airstream Argosy Owner's group on Facebook and read all I could about this short-lived Airstream model. I went to the group's items-for-sale section and read every listing. A handful had been up for a year or more and the owners didn't reply to messages. Some were sold and the seller hadn't removed the listing. Others were not the right layout or size, too expensive, or too far away. The group itself was a wealth of information and it was amazing to see how people had fixed up their Argosys to suit their needs, wants, and tastes. There were Argosys that were restored to their original colors, and others painted in bright primary color schemes. Some even had custom murals.

Potential campers can show up in group feeds on Facebook. For example, these five photos of a 1972 20-foot Argosy were in a post in which the owner was trying to gauge interest by potential buyers.

Now we can go back to this story: One day, a post with five photos of a 1972 20-foot Argosy popped up in my Facebook feed. The owner was trying to decide whether to sell.

"Let me know if you're interested," he posted, and I wrote to him right away. I wasn't the first to respond to the owner Travis, but I'm guessing I was one of the more persistent. I sent Travis questions that he patiently answered. I kept looking at the five little pictures of this little camper in his post—and the more I did, the more I wanted it. And the more I wanted it, the more anxiety I had about making an offer—what if I offered too much? How much is this thing really worth? What if I do the wrong thing and it turns out to be crap?

It was obvious that there was work to be done. I told myself over and over that if other people could do it, I could. I don't know that I actually believed it, but I kept telling myself that.

A few days later, I told Travis I was ready to make an offer. And, just my luck, he replied that someone else had already beat me to it the previous day, and had made an offer he had accepted. I was devastated. And annoyed with myself that I'd already forgotten about lesson number one.

A few months of searching and inquiring and looking at for-sale campers went by, and I was becoming increasingly discouraged. I half-heartedly responded to an advertisement for a rare 1950s Wally Byam Holiday, designed and produced by the same person who founded the Airstream company. I knew of that camper's rarity and history, and knew that it would take dedication and a lot of time and work to restore it to its original state. The asking price was more than reasonable. I figured that it would be gone by the time I saw it, but it turns out that I was the first to respond to the listing.

The seller enthusiastically sent me several emails and photos, and after a few exchanges, I was excited about the prospect of owning the Holiday. I told him I was 99.9999 percent sure I wanted it, but I'd need to come see it in person to make an offer. He agreed. Then, a couple of days before the day we agreed to meet, he sent me an email saying he wanted me to call him to "clear some things up" for me about vintage trailers. When I called, he told me he had sold it to someone else because he felt they appreciated the value and history of the camper much more than I would be able to, and they would treat it with the respect and attention it deserves. But, he said, he'd be more than willing to sell me one of his other travel trailers.

If you're curious about the Wally Byam Holiday, Airstream Inc. features this article about its history on its company blog. [airstream.com/blog/wally-byams-holiday]

Um, no.

Whether his condescension was intentional or not, it was the straw that broke my back. I was sick of the back and forth, excitement and disappointment, scams and attitudes and frustrations over the last couple of years. It turns out, I thought, that this vintage camper business is not for me.

Since he had been so helpful and basically the exact opposite of Mr. Condescension, I decided to reach out to Travis again to thank him for all of his time and information, and let him know that I was happy his Argosy had found a good home. To my surprise, he replied and told me that the previous potential buyer had backed out of the purchase, and he hadn't had time to list it for sale again. The offer Travis had accepted was less than what he'd originally asked, and he said he would accept that amount from me, too, if I still wanted it.

Uh, yeah! I told him that I wanted to talk to him on the phone to make sure he was a real person. I didn't want to lose out on getting the camper, so while talking to him (yes, he is a real person), I agreed to purchase the little Argosy.

What I did next was risky: I paid for the Argosy sight-unseen. Travis didn't ask me to and said I didn't have to—and happens to be a man of his word, but I didn't know that yet. I was scared that someone would buy it before I was able to get there to pick it up, and I didn't want to deal with more disappointment. Of course, when I paid for it, I was scared that I'd get there and there wouldn't be any camper, or it would be completely trashed, and pretty much every other horrific scenario that I'd heard about from others. I knew I was risking becoming one of those people buying a nonexistent camper from a creepy scammer, and I didn't tell anyone what I did because I knew it wasn't the smartest thing I'd ever done. Thankfully, Travis is a great guy and I got a good deal, but I still feel a snippet of embarrassment that I was impulsive about the payment. Travis graciously overnighted the bill of sale and title so I was able to register the camper and have a license plate to take with me on the trip.

Holy cow, I finally owned a frickin' camper! There was just one little logistical detail I needed to take care of: I live in Vermont and the travel trailer lived in Missouri. There was the additional little detail that my current vehicle wouldn't tow it. I looked into uShip, a service in which freelance drivers bid on hauling items for people, but some of the quotes were higher than the cost of the camper and I couldn't justify that.

I spotted a used F150 with a tow package at a nearby dealer, drove there, did a test drive, traded in my Jeep, and brought the truck home that same day. When I pulled in the driveway with my new-to-me truck, I think that was the first time Dwayne realized that this whole camper thing wasn't just a phase I was going through—I'd been going through phases my whole life, if you listened to

My sister Lois and I went to Missouri to get the Argosy. It was my first time hauling a camper, and I was pleasantly surprised at how easy it was.

my mom make excuses for my pre-30ish behavior. And she was right—the half-shaved head inspired by Cindy Lauper, the dressing-in-all-black, and wearing men's vintage silk pajama bottoms as pants were three of many phases I'm glad to have survived relatively scar-free. But when you bring home a truck with a 36-gallon tank and a heavy duty tow package, it's difficult to deny the plausibility of a camper in the future, no matter how phase-y your life has been.

Within a handful of days, I was off to Missouri. My sister Lois joined me for the trip. It took two days to get there, which gave me plenty of time to play out possible worst-case scenarios in my head: What if this guy is ripping me off? What if I get a flat tire on the way home? What if I can't tow it? What if it's stolen? What if my husband hates it? What if *I* hate it?!? Am I crazy? What if this is just a phase I'm going through?!?

It turns out that Travis wasn't ripping me off, and he wasn't a creepy scammer. He'd been transparent with me and told me what he knew about the camper's condition. He had put on new tires

Inside the Argosy, looking toward the back.

(that I had paid for ahead of time) and greased her bearings so that my trip home would be less stressful. He walked me through and around, showing me how things worked, what things didn't work, and what things he wasn't sure of. He had put all of the pieces and parts he had taken out back inside of the camper and it looked a bit ramshackle because of this, but I was prepared for that because of his photos. The propane tanks had long since been removed, and that was fine since I didn't intend to use propane. He had included an extra set of curtains his wife had made, and an almost-new space heater. He went through the quirks of the camper, like how to close and open the door with its broken handle (vice grips!) and how to fold the step up and down.

With Travis's help, I got hitched up and plugged in. After a lights check and mirror adjustment, Lois and I were off, on our way back home with a planned camping stop in Indiana the first night, and in Ohio the second.

I had reserved a pull-through space at a campground because I didn't want to have to back up. So many people in online forums and in person had expressed their disdain and fears of backing up that I just assumed I wouldn't be able to do it without making an ass of myself and smashing the camper into a tree or deer or person. (Side note: It's not difficult, it simply needs practice.)

After we parked in our spot, we got out of the truck and opened the camper door to find that the refrigerator had fallen over and several loose Argosy pieces had scattered around inside the camper. After we struggled to get the fridge back in place (they are small, but painfully heavy!), we got plugged in. With the exception of an annoying buzzing sound, things seemed to be working.

We turned on a couple of the inside lights, and Lois suggested we turn on the space heater Travis had included. The heater ran for a few minutes before we heard a pop and the power went out. I had no clue yet about the infamous unreliability of old Univolt converters. All I could figure out at the time was that whatever that buzzing sound was probably had something to do with the power being on, because now the annoying buzzing was off and the power was off. I had no manual and no knowledge about how to troubleshoot it, so we were power-free for the remainder of the trip.

The front gaucho bed was clear enough to sleep on, and I let Lois have that for the night. Since the side gaucho was covered in Argosy bits and pieces, I decided to sleep on the floor. Thankfully I brought my heavy duty down sleeping bag because it was a cold night. It wasn't cold enough to keep the resident mice from making noises, but it was enough to convince me that we should spend the next night in a hotel rather than a campground.

It didn't occur to me until I actually needed fuel that when I was towing something, I would have to approach gas stations strategically so that I had plenty of room to maneuver. I'd never noticed before how gas pumps are often situated in a pattern that makes it difficult to pull through with a camper or are too close to the accompanying store to be able to pull forward. Diesel pumps tend to have room for big vehicles to maneuver through, but my F150 runs on regular gas. The first time entering a gas station while towing Zola, I "strategically" went through the last pump aisle thinking it would give me enough clearance. But I pulled too close, and when I was leaving, I almost hit the

Once we got the refrigerator back in place with bungees to hold it, we were able to get settled in for the night. Lois slept on the front gaucho, and I slept on the floor. That's the kind of sister I am.

barrier that keeps people from running into the pump. When I was about two millimeters away, and had gotten out to stare at it wondering what to do, a man who was leaving the station store asked if he could help.

"I do this all the time," he said, explaining that he worked in a boat yard. Normally it's against all instincts to hand a stranger my keys to my new-to-me truck that's pulling my new-to-me Airstream, but he did as promised and expertly redirected Zola away from the pole and back to safety.

Lois and I got home safe and mostly sound. One of the front curved banana wraps had come loose because it was attached to rotted wood (you can see that in the picture at the beginning of this

On our second night on the way home, Lois and I stayed in a hotel. Luckily, it was near the 8 Sisters Bakery so we could load up on carbs before the day's drive.

chapter) and had to be bungeed to the trailer to avoid it getting ripped off. All the windows stayed intact, and we avoided flat tires and additional dents.

Dwayne didn't say too much of anything about it. Even though he'd humored me by going on camper tours, I knew that he had no desire to be a camper owner. I silently convinced myself that I would be able to convert him eventually.

What I didn't realize was that Dwayne had a better idea of just how much of a project I had in front of me, and understandably had his doubts that I would follow through with it due to my lack of skills. I had a lot to prove, and a lot of work to do.

I had no idea how much of an understatement that was.

Long-distance camper shopping

What can you do if a camper is too far away to check out in person—send your money out into the ether and hope for the best? Well, yeah, that can work out, but it isn't the top recommendation. Even with the happy ending to my story, I would still urge you to do your best to see any travel trailer you want to buy in person if you can. I had considered flying out to look at mine first; I can't recall why I didn't do that. I also tried repeatedly to get an inspector through the Air Forums volunteer inspector network, but didn't receive a reply to my messages. Here are some more options:

- Ask the owner if they are willing to do a Facetime or Zoom call with you in order to give you a live virtual tour. Zack's sellers graciously did this for me. Be prepared with specific questions.
- Check to see if there are any legitimate vintage travel trailer restorers or renovators in the area in which your prospective purchase is located. Sometimes they are willing to go check out a camper for you for a fee, and give you an objective opinion about the trailer's condition. If you trust a restorer in one area of the country but your potential camper is in another area, ask the restorer if they can take a look at photos and videos of the camper for you for a fee. If the camper owner is willing to take a video or photos of more than they put in their listing, that's information that can be shared with the restorer, too.
- If you have a friend near the camper's location, ask them if they would go look at it and get a feel for things. Ask them to take pictures and to Facetime or Zoom with you so that you can get the views you want.
- Ask people you've met in a camper forum or club if anyone close to the camper location would be willing to go check it out for you.

CRYSTAL MCCULLOUGH

Zack (formerly Gus) on the way home from Michigan.

5

FINDING OLD CAMPERS FOR SALE

NOW THAT YOU'RE ACTIVELY STARTING YOUR SEARCH, where are all the for-sale campers for you to pick from? Thankfully, you can often find campers for sale in the same place(s) you go to in order to learn about them, like clubs, online forums, and classified advertisements. While these might not have the same number of travel trailers for sale as they once did, they are still the best places to start. Here are a few resources.

The Airstream Club International—formerly known as the Wally Byam Caravan Club International— has an intra-club (a club within a club), The Vintage Airstream Club. Airstream rallies often include members of both.

Vintage camper club sites and forums. One of the best places to find out about campers is to visit and join both generic vintage/classic club web sites and specific-brand camper club sites. For example, Tin Can Tourists is a century-old organization whose members own campers and motorhomes from nearly every brand from every decade. Its buy/sell area of the site is accessible to all, whether you're a member or not. [tincantourists.com] The National Serro Scotty Organization (NSSO) is an incredible resource for those interested in Scotty travel trailers, with in-depth history, photos, and information about rebuilds and restorations. [nationalserroscotty.org]

Sometimes campers come to you, if people know you're interested. I ended up with this Shasta Daisy after its previous owner pulled into my driveway with it to ask me about my Argosy.

Facebook interest groups. Name a brand of travel trailer and you'll probably find a group on Facebook dedicated to it. Some require that you should already be an owner of the kind of camper the group is about, while other groups welcome anyone and everyone who has an interest in their make/model/pastime. Examples include the Apache Camper Preservation Society [facebook.com/groups/201182856613333] and Classic Winnebagos & Vintage RVs [facebook.com/groups/247948994619].

Facebook marketplace selling groups. There are countless vintage camper selling groups on Facebook, as well as its general Marketplace. You can start with a simple search for 'vintage camper' within groups to find both generic and specific-brand selling groups.

You'll often see vintage and classic campers for sale at rallies. Many of them, like this 1948 Spartan Manor, have been restored and listed at a price that reflects its improvements.

Facebook camper location-based groups. These groups are basically the same as the two previous Facebook groups, except that they are limited to a certain state or area. For example, in my area, there are a few camper swap/for sale groups that cover both newish and oldish campers. There is a private group called New England and Beyond Vintage Campers that only allows people from the area to join. It allows for-sale posts of vintage campers and motorhomes in the area. [facebook.com/groups/NewEnglandandBeyondVintageCampers]

Camper rallies. There are camper rallies all over the United States, and many are vintage and/or classic only. Rallies almost always have an open house a day or two at the event, so you can walk around the rally site and take a look around and inside the campers open for viewing. The owner is

BEFORE YOU BUY A VINTAGE CAMPER

Once in a great while you'll come upon a small field of campers on the roadside, like this one in Alfred, ME.

usually there during the open house, and it's an ideal opportunity to ask them about their specific experience with their camper.

There are often campers for sale at rallies. This is a great way to get a feel for prices in the area and what to expect when looking for a particular model/year.

To find rallies near you, look in club newsletters and magazines. A couple of starter resources include *Vintage Camper Trailer Magazine*'s rally site [vintagetrailerrallies.com], and Tin Can Tourists' events page [tincantourists.com/events]. Many Facebook groups hold their own rallies.

On the side of the road, in random fields, etc. Depending on where you live, a simple drive around the area can yield sightings of vintage and classic campers for sale on someone's front lawn

There's something about a little vintage camper all alone in a field that makes me want to take it home.

or seemingly not being used sitting in a field or behind a barn. Knocking on the owner's door and asking them about their camper, even if it's not for sale, can sometimes be a fruitful way to learn more and potentially purchase a camper that caught your attention. Be sure to be respectful of owners and their property—for example, no uninvited peeking in camper windows.

    I've gotten leads on travel trailers from people who have stopped in because they saw me working on one of the campers outside, or someone told them they thought I might know a thing or two about old campers. They had an old travel trailer for sale and they were wondering if I knew anyone who might be interested. Or, they had a friend who had a friend who had an old camper, and would I be interested in it?

Other camping or activity clubs. Some camping clubs have a for-sale section of their site. For example, Sisters on the Fly has a marketplace where members can list their campers for sale. Many of them are classic and vintage. [sistersonthefly.com/sotf-marketplace]

Renovators and restorers. I almost didn't include this resource since every legit, quality renovator and restorer I know of is so busy with client projects that they don't have spare time to answer our long emails or phone calls full of questions. I recommend going to their site or social media pages to find out if they have anything for sale. Some renovators and restorers who have inventory will sell their vintage campers as-is for those wanting to do their own work, or will put you on their schedule to renovate/restore their for-sale campers. For example, Flyte Camp in Bend, Oregon sells campers both as-is and built out to your specifications [flytecamp.com/vintage-trailer-sales]. Heintz Designs in Panama City, Florida does the same. [heintzdesigns.com]

Vintage camper magazines. *Vintage Camper Trailers Magazine* not only has a print publication, it also hosts several vintage camper rallies and the Vintage Camper Bootcamp, a four-day camper-renovation intensive held every spring in California. *Trailer Life*, in publication since 1941, generally covers current campers, but also has coverage of vintage trailer rallies, renovations, and lifestyles. [www.trailerlife.com] *Vintage Trailer Magazine* has limited listings for sale, but is worth it for the photos. [vintagetrailermagazine.com]

Vintage Camper Trailer Magazine
photo courtesy of Vintage Camper Trailer Magazine

Camper classifieds. Little Vintage Trailer lists vintage trailers for sale on the home page of its site. [littlevintagetrailer.com] Airstream Classifieds lists both old and newer Airstreams for sale. [airstreamclassifieds.com] Airstream Hunter Marketplace lists tons of newish, classic, and vintage

Airstreams. [marketplace.airstreamhunter.com/] *Vintage Camper Trailers Magazine* has an extensive classifieds section. [classifieds.vintagecampertrailers.com] Tin Can Tourists, as mentioned earlier, also has classified ads for old trailers.

craigslist and eBay. Both of these veteran selling sites often have several vintage and classic options available. [craigslist.org and ebay.com] You can use web sites like Search all of Craigslist [searchcraigslist.org] that will search—as you might guess—all of the locations of craigslist for what you are looking for.

6

HOW MUCH IS THIS OLD CAMPER WORTH?

HOW DO YOU KNOW what a camper is worth? The short answer to this question is "It's worth what someone is willing to pay for it." That's a nice, convenient, and realistic answer for many people, since if you finally found THE camper you've always wanted, no matter its pedigree, you're more likely to be willing to pay a higher price to get it. It took me awhile to learn that "worth," "value," and "price" are different things, even though they are often used interchangeably. The

This 17-foot 1968 Aristocrat was for sale at the Enchanted Trail campground in Albuquerque, New Mexico—a must-stop if you're travelling Route 66.

terms 'book price,' 'market price,' and 'insurance replacement value' are all based on standard formulas that have been determined by various expert organizations and insurance companies. A price is determined by the seller, and they can pick whatever number they want to start at.

For the most part, travel trailer prices are all over the map, and as a buyer, you're responsible for determining your budget. You might want a rare or uncommon vintage camper and be willing to pay good money for one of them no matter how much work they need. Or you might want to buy new or a newer-used camper with as few issues as possible that you can take straight to a campsite. As for sellers, some (probably most) want to make as much money as they can on a sale, and others

BEFORE YOU BUY A VINTAGE CAMPER

Another camper for sale at the same campground. In hindsight, I probably should have purchased this Fireball—but I'd have a lot less to write about.

that want a camper to go to a good home and are willing to negotiate. And then there are all the buyers and sellers in between.

Perceived value is in the eyes of the beholder

Does perceived value mean anything? The short answer is *yes*. The caveat, though, is that everybody has a different interpretation of perception.

I occasionally haul campers for people, and a couple of years ago, I offered to bring a 31-foot Airstream from the Detroit area to Quartzite, Arizona for a friend. Before I left, I spent time online

The inside rustic/Western theme of the 1974 Mobile Traveler.

looking for a unique camper for sale in Arizona that I could potentially buy and haul back home to Vermont to fix, flip, or rent. If it was in good-enough shape, I could stay in it on the way home.

I checked out sites where I've often found vintage trailers for sale—Tin Can Tourists, Facebook Marketplace, Facebook groups, craigslist, eBay, Airstream Classifieds, Airstream Hunter, and Little Vintage Trailer to start, and didn't have any luck. Then I remembered that a camping group I belonged to had a camper-for-sale area on its site, and I went through the 50 or so trailers listed. I was losing hope that I'd find anything until I got to the very last listing: a 1974 Mobile Traveler that was owned by the group's founder—and it happened to be in the Phoenix area. Wow, wouldn't it be cool to own a camper that the founder of this group owned? Wouldn't members on the East Coast be super eager to rent it from me? It had upcycled and vintage furniture and decor, and seemed like a win-win. The price was high compared to other campers like it, but I after sitting down with a calculator, I was convinced it would pay for itself within an acceptable amount of time, and then be a regular source of income by renting it through Outdoorsy.

The Mobile Traveler's newly designed interior had a cute theme, a vintage copper sink, homemade rustic cupboards, a new mattress and bed platform, and the bonus of having a small bathroom with a new toilet. The money from its sale would go to a nonprofit organization that had a mission I admired. No one had used it since it had been redone.

While in Arizona, I found a 1974 Mobile Traveler for sale that had been renovated and redecorated inside and out. It had a few quirks—missing some trim, overall hail damage, no safety chains (the seller added them before I left), and the door lock didn't work—but the whole thing appeared solid. To me, its story increased its value. It had spent years as a coffee klatsch on a ranch in Colorado.

If I see a camper for sale that piques my curiosity, I search for the same model and year of camper to see what they are selling or have sold for. I look through model-specific forums to see the prices people are asking. I check out any online groups or classified ads that list that kind of camper for sale. I ask people who own the same kind of camper to see what they think it would be worth, and what issues they've had with their camper. I wasn't able to find information on Mobile Travelers, though, other than some of its manufacturing history.

I contacted the owner and made arrangements to come see the camper a day before I was going to leave Arizona and head home. I inspected the Mobile Traveler and it appeared to be in good

My dog Dawkins and I camped in the Mobile Traveler on the way home to Vermont. All went smoothly for the first couple of days.

shape, albeit largely unremarkable. There was no water damage, the frame was solid, and there was no mold/mildew/rot in any of the usual places. It was missing a few pieces of trim, missing safety chains, the main door lock didn't work, and it had all-over hail damage. All the windows were original and intact. It had been painted with a Navajo-inspired design on the curb side, and a mountain/lake/eagle mural on the street side. It had its share of Arizona red dust both in and outside, but otherwise was clean. It had a new mattress and bedding, and included several decorative and practical items, including a small propane cooktop and dishes.

    The seller was asking $6,000. Even though I hadn't been able to find out much about the camper or how much others sold for, I was pretty sure it wasn't worth that by the books. But since its sale

The tail/brake lights stopped working on the road. I always carry temporary magnetic lights for this reason. I fixed them when I got home.

was for a good cause and I was excited to have it as a future rental, I made a counteroffer of $5,000 that she accepted. We arranged for me to pick it up in the morning, and as part of our deal, she would arrange to have safety chains welded on and get the sale paperwork together.

The first two days on the road from Arizona to Vermont were fine. The chairs moved around because they weren't attached to anything, so I used a couple of bungee cords to attach them to the table that was attached to the wall to hold them in place. On the third day, however, after driving a long day and looking forward to supper and sleep, I opened up the camper door and was welcomed with what looked like a crime scene. I seriously thought someone had broken in when I wasn't looking and tossed the place. The table had come unscrewed from the wall, had fallen over, and part of

It turns out that the Mobile Traveler was not rebuilt with mobile traveling in mind.

its trim came off. The chairs were toppled. The rustic handmade wall cupboard that I thought was so cool was broken and hanging by one screw—it had been attached only to 1/4 inch Luan plywood rather than a wall stud, and the other three screws had created three large holes where they moved back and forth and then tore out. The broken cupboard had swung down and smashed into the counter that the sink was in, which in turn broke the counter away from the wall and broke it into non-fixable pieces.

After I realized it wasn't a break in, I knew that the issue was that this camper was rebuilt as if it would never move—as if it were a stick-built house on a foundation, not a living space that regularly hits potholes. A camper's parts and contents have to be compatible with road travel if it's going to be used successfully as intended. Who knows, this camper may have been perfectly fine if it had

BEFORE YOU BUY A VINTAGE CAMPER

I couldn't wait to get this experience behind me.

never moved, with the exception of the cupboard—it was heavy on its own, and storing anything in it would only cause the weight to increase and put pressure on the screw attachment. In any case, it had seemed sturdy when I looked it over, and I never remotely considered the possibility of it self-destructing on the way home.

My perception of its value dropped. I sent the seller a text to tell her what happened, and asked if I could get a partial refund even though I had purchased the camper "as-is." Even though the workmanship of the rebuild has been done by the seller and those she hired to help, buying a travel trailer as-is means that the seller is off the hook if something isn't in working condition. Most travel trailer sales are as-is, just like in the used car market. Since I bought as-is, I was the party responsible for any repairs and expenses. Still, I figured it was worth a try to ask. She suggested I bring it back and she

Finally home, for better or worse.

would give me my money back minus $1,000—which may not seem fair, but technically she didn't even have to reply to my text.

I considered her offer, but by then I was closer to Vermont than Arizona and I had a schedule I had to stick to, so this wasn't a feasible solution. I kept on heading east, and Dawkins and I stayed in hotels for the remainder of the trip since it was impossible to get around in the travel trailer safely. It was snowy and icy when I finally got home. When I was backing the camper up into its place in the driveway, the truck slid and gave a good smack to one of the camper's front corners, denting it and lowering its literal and perceived value even more. I got out of the truck, went into the house, and left the camper and truck blocking the driveway until my husband got home. I was tired, pissed, and ready to pay someone to haul it away.

BEFORE YOU BUY A VINTAGE CAMPER

After the Mobile Traveler got home, repairs and rebuilding began, keeping in mind its original simplicity and theme. Here's a new oak countertop in place. If you look closely, on the right you can see a couple of the scrapes and a hole on the wall that the old pantry cabinet caused when it fell off.

Once I calmed down, I got to work fixing and rebuilding the interior. I put in new shelving, a new counter built by my grand-nephew Lowell, new structurally sound storage, a mini-fridge, better external lighting, new wiring, and so on, getting it ready to rent during the next camping season. I made sure that its weight distribution was set up how it should be. I put it up on Outdoorsy and waited for the rental inquiries to come in.

Weeks went by and it received *no* interest as a rental. None. By this time I was calling the camper *Gretta* since it continually went out of its way to remind me that I should re*gret* its purchase.

In the fall, I decided to put it up for sale. A lot of people came around to kick the tires, and many told me they were in love with its layout and design. But no one seemed to agree with me that part

I took this 1967 Banner in partial trade for the Mobile Traveler, and sold it to my sister Diane. She called it "the ugly blue camper" when she saw photos of it, but when she saw it in person, she loved it. She has since made some needed fixes, painted it inside and out, and redecorated to make it hers.

of its value lay in the camper's story. I was willing to take a financial hit because even though I'd begrudgingly loved it in its revitalized state, I was ready to move on to other more satisfying projects. It obviously wasn't meant to belong to me.

After several months, a buyer finally came along that was beyond excited about the Mobile Traveler's history as well as its current repaired/updated condition. I was transparent with her about my 'adventures' with the camper, and she was still ecstatic. The perceived value was more important to her than a book value. She even liked the dent I'd put in the front—it told a story, she said. I agreed to take her 1967 Banner as $500 toward the Mobile Traveler's price, and my sister Diane bought the

Banner from me for what I paid for it. I lost money, time, and some sanity overall, but the buyer of the Mobile traveler and Diane's excitement made all the hassle worth it.

Appraisals

To really get an idea of what a camper is worth on the open and collector's markets, it's well worth paying for a professional appraisal. This service costs a few hundred dollars, but is priceless when you want to sell, and for purchasing replacement-value insurance (most companies will only reimburse you for what you paid for a vintage travel trailer rather than what it's now worth). I had my small Argosy appraised by Tim Heintz of Heintz Designs. [heintzdesigns.com] Polk Associates also appraises vintage and classic campers. [polkassociates-llc.com] Reach out to either to find out how to have a camper appraised virtually.

If the camper you're buying or selling has a low price point, or obviously needs a great deal of work, getting an appraisal isn't necessarily a worthwhile investment.

Blue books

Tin Can Tourists has its own blue book, a database of for-sale and sold campers, and shows you the price at which they were listed. It's probable that some of these sold for less than the listing prices shown in the database, but it's a great way to get a feel for prices around the country. [tincantourists.com/vintage-trailer-bluebook]

NADA Guides has a database of campers to search through, although it is limited to camper brands that are still sold today (i.e. Airstream, Shasta, and Winnebago) and not all years and model information is available. Still, it's worth a shot to see if a camper you're interested in is listed. [nadaguides.com/RVs]

Campers at the annual Brattleboro, Vermont KOA fall rally.

7

CAMPER UNICORNS

ONCE IN A GREAT WHILE one of those I-can't-believe-it camper unicorn deals comes along. A couple of summers ago when I was outside working on my little Argosy, a person stopped by to tell me he knew someone who was selling an Airstream Argosy like mine, and he wondered if I would be interested in buying it. The seller was going to scrap it if it didn't get out of his way soon. I didn't need another Argosy, but it's difficult for me to turn down the chance to look at another one since

I try to look for all the bad things about a camper first.

they are few and far between in these parts. I have people ask me all the time if I can help them find a camper, and this might be one I could buy and flip, or buy and fix, or use for parts for my or my sister Lois and brother-in-law Russell's Argosy.

I asked Russell if he'd go with me to look at it, and we set off on a couple-hour drive to its location. The seller took us out to a relatively unused part of his large property, and there was his Argosy sitting in a deserted dirt pit. He invited us to take our time and look around.

I noticed the bad things first: one of the hard-to-find front curved windows was missing. These windows can cost from $600 to $900 to replace, if you can find one. In its place was a broken piece of plastic. I walked around it and took note of the broken lights and a couple of holes in the aluminum. It had a padlock on the door that someone had added for security. I noted that it had an intact awning, so that was a potential check on the good side. Its jack was gone and there was no air conditioner. I took pictures for us to look at later.

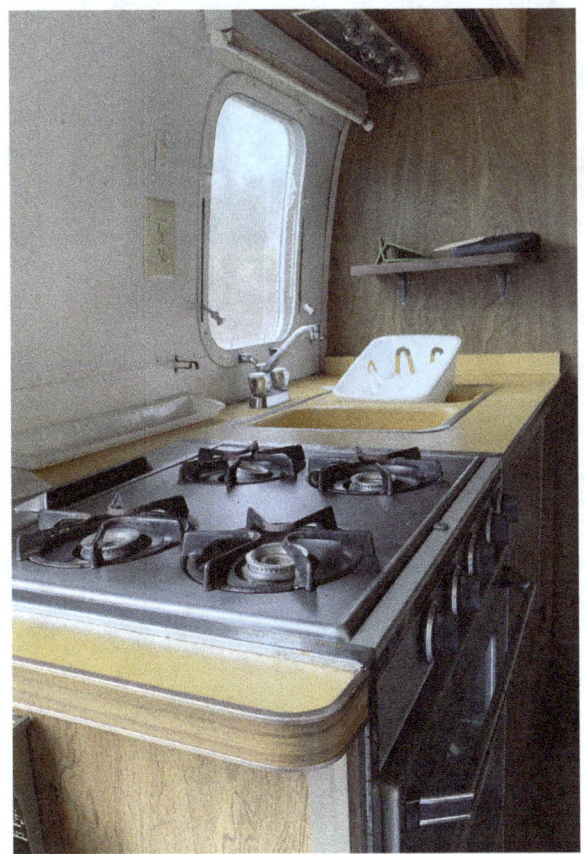

This Argosy was like a time capsule.

Even though it hadn't been used in years, this Argosy's 46-year-old systems still worked. It was like a time capsule inside.

When we went inside, I was blown away. This 1974 Argosy was a time capsule on the inside, with the exception of the corner under the broken window that had rotted and caved in from long-time water exposure. A little of the vinyl on the cabinets had started peeling, likely from the same moisture. But there were no musty or cat-pee smells. I couldn't find any nests or poop or other evidence of rodents. There were no water stains in the usual places. I don't think anyone had ever used the toilet, tub, or oven. It was top-of-the-line 1974 through and through, with extras like built-in speakers throughout and an 8-track tape player. All of the light fixtures looked clean and new and had all of their parts.

I listened to Russell talk to the seller about how we were looking for a parts camper to help rebuild our current Argosys. But after seeing the inside, I pulled Russell aside and suggested that he should buy this one to fix up and use, and use his other one as the parts Argosy rather than the other way around since this one was in so much better condition. I threw in that I would love to have the awning if I could. He agreed, and went back to talk to the seller.

It even had the original stereo system, featuring an 8-track tape player and cassette player.

At the time of this writing, I'd venture to guess that this Argosy would be priced anywhere from $3,000 to $6,000 on craigslist or Facebook Marketplace, depending on its location. I was calculating what I could pay and what the awning was worth, and what it could be flipped for when Russell blurted out an offer.

"Would you take $500?" asked Russell. I braced myself, assuming that the seller would break out laughing or swearing, but instead, he said "yes," but that he'd have to check with his son who co-owned it with him. When we went to his office to talk details, the seller's son walked in and gruffly told me that he wanted $600. I agreed to the $600 because it still was an insanely good deal, and didn't want the son to back out. We shook hands.

Lois and Russell's 26-foot Argosy after a good washing. Russell is priming and painting the steel endcaps in this photo. It needed a new jack, a new front curved window (which they already had), and a couple of patches, but otherwise was ready to go camping.

The next day we went back to pick up the Argosy. With an exchange of cash, a bill of sale, and another handshake, Russell and Lois were the owners of a 1974 26′ center twin/rear bath for the enviable price of $600. I purchased my two Argosys for $2,500 and $4,000 respectively, and I thought those were great prices! And they were, because I was looking for these two models specifically, so that made them worth it to me. But I'm still jealous!

Making an offer

I wish every single camper sale-price negotiation went as well as Lois and Russell's. There are people who, like the previous owner of their camper, simply want to get the camper out of the way. They might have gotten it in trade toward something else even if they didn't care for camping, or they bought property that had the old thing parked on it already. I've heard plenty of stories of people asking the owners if they are interested in getting rid of a camper, and the owner telling them to just take it, or letting them take it for a nominal price. The worst they can say is "no."

Lois and Russell were able to take their travel trailer camping not long after they got it. They named it Jude after the song they first danced to together.

Usually an active seller has a price in mind, and also has an absolute low price they are willing to consider. Sometimes prices are listed as 'firm,' meaning that's the lowest the seller states they will accept. Sometimes these prices are fair, sometimes not. It might work to offer a lower number, but the seller may hold out for someone who will match their price.

I can't give you a definitive formula to come up with a number to offer a particular seller since there are so many variables in every sale. You can ask what they want for it, take a copy of your checklist with you when you go look it over, make an offer that works for you and doesn't break your budget, and—you guessed it—the worse they can say is "no."

Another photo inside Lois and Russell's unicorn.

8

KICKING THE TIRES

OK. IT'S TIME to go look at your potential camper. From a distance, it seems like just what you were looking for, but you still want to see it in person to make sure that it meets your needs. The owner tells you they have had a lot of offers, so there's pressure to act fast if it's something you want. The owner is willing to negotiate, and they'd like you to come by today to look at it.

Before heading out, there are a few questions you'll need to have answers for. Some of these are the necessary red-tape bits and pieces that you'll need to legally and safely become a camper owner. Others are suggested items to look into, and could be less of a hassle to get them done or to know the answers before setting out to buy.

- Does your state require a title, and for what time span? Some states don't require a title to register a camper that is over a certain number of years old. They may require a bill of sale. Ask your department of motor vehicles registration department.
- Do you need a travel permit to move a camper without being registered? The DMV should also have this information.
- What kind of working external lights are required to be on the road legally? This information is usually easily accessible on your state's web site.
- Does your state require that the camper has a trailer brake? This should be on the same state website.
- Can your vehicle tow it safely? Just because its specs say it can haul 5,000 pounds doesn't mean that it can do it safely.
- Can you park your trailer in your neighborhood? Some homeowners associations and zoning rules won't allow a camper to sit on your front lawn or in your driveway. Check with your HOA or area zoning-planning office.
- What kind of payment is the seller asking for? Cash? Bank check? PayPal? Venmo? Are they asking for a deposit or a hold fee?

Things to bring with you

- Folding ladder. Ideally you want a lightweight aluminum stand-alone ladder that will allow you to see the top of the camper.
- Camera (phone camera is fine). You'll want to take as many photos as possible to remind yourself what you looked at.
- Flashlight. To check out dark and hidden areas that might otherwise be difficult to see.

BEFORE YOU BUY A VINTAGE CAMPER

Always bring a camera with you and take plenty of pictures.

- Tape measure. In case you need to measure anything.
- Safety stuff. Gloves, in case you have to touch something gross. Safety glasses for looking in questionable places.
- Generator. If the seller isn't close enough to a power source for you to plug in.
- Extension cord. In case the seller doesn't have one for you to use with the generator or their power source.
- A friend. Having someone with you can make it feel less awkward going to a stranger's place to look at a camper, especially if it's off the beaten path. Of course, the seller could be awesome and trustworthy, but it doesn't hurt to err on the side of caution, especially if you're carrying a bunch of cash to pay them in case you decide you want to buy.

I have yet to have an air conditioner or refrigerator work even though the previous owner said that the previous owner said it worked. Try as many systems as you can before buying.

Inspecting the camper

You arrive at the address the owner gave to you, and you see the camper parked out in the back field. Looks good from a distance, and hopefully what you see (and smell) up close is just as good.

Depending on the owner/seller, they might have some alternative facts or exaggerations about the camper's abilities and features. You don't have to walk into the situation full of mistrust and suspicion, but you should definitely keep in mind that the person selling is trying to, you know, sell you something.

Even the most trustworthy and experienced sellers will occasionally use the phrase "I've never used it/turned it on, but the previous owner said it worked." I've heard it in regard to water pumps, brakes, lights, refrigerators, air conditioners, hot water heaters, furnaces, and door locks. Now, maybe it worked for the previous owner when they owned it, or maybe the previous owner hadn't tried anything or turned anything on but the previous-previous owner said it worked.

Your options are limited: believe them and hope for the best, don't believe them and hope for the best, or arrange to test systems when you are there. The latter option can take a lot of time, and a seller may not be that keen on going through hooking up the camper to electricity, water, and propane. The propane tanks could be empty, and they likely won't have extra tanks hanging around to test the stove. If the camper has been sitting around, it probably doesn't have water in the tank, and its battery will be dead if it wasn't maintained over time.

Here's a very typical potential buyer/potential seller conversation:
"Does the A/C work?"
"I haven't tried it, but the previous owner said it worked."
"Does the stove work?"
"I don't know, but the previous owner said it worked."
"How about the fridge?"
"Well, I haven't used it, but the previous owner said it worked."

Now, just imagine this for nearly everything in a camper that at some point should have functioned. The water heater. The toilet, shower, and sink. The fan. The furnace. The water pump. 12v and 110 electrical wiring. Marker, directional, and brake lights. Even the door lock.

Functioning appliances and working electrical and water systems are a bonus with many old campers. I have purchased both campers that have them and campers that don't. Saying "I haven't tried it but the previous owner said it worked" could very well be the entire truth and nothing but the truth, but it's not helpful information.

There are most likely two electrical systems in the camper: 12 volt (DC off-a-battery current) and 110 volt (AC household current). Unless its electrical system has been greatly updated, you won't be able to run anything with AC power if you're not plugged into a power source. If the battery is dead, you won't be able to turn on 12-volt items such as lights, a ceiling fan, or the water pump.

In my experience, it's highly unlikely that a seller will charge up the battery, plug in to shore power, fill up the propane and water tank, prime the water system, and so on just so a potential

If the current owner says that the fridge in their camper works, ask them to turn it on a couple of hours before you get there. Camper fridges can take awhile to cool down. (AS)

buyer can see if and how everything works. On the other hand, it wouldn't hurt to ask to see the camper set up and working if they are claiming one or all of those systems are functional. Either the seller will or they won't, but in my book, they are more likely to get a solid offer if I can see what works and what doesn't—and it would probably help their sales potential overall. And asking to see systems in action shows the seller that you are a serious buyer, not just there for the heck of it.

Let's assume that this won't happen. At least you can check a handful of things without the camper being fully prepped and plugged in.

If your vehicle has the same plug as the camper (a four pin or seven pin), ask if you can back up to it and plug in to check the directional and brake lights. You don't need to do a full hook-up to do

BEFORE YOU BUY A VINTAGE CAMPER

Ask the owner if you can hook the camper up to your vehicle to see if its running lights and brake lights/turn signals work.

that, just plug into your vehicle. Turn on the light controls in your vehicle to see what setting sends power to the cord.

Before you leave home, ask the owner if they have a power source close enough to plug the camper in. If they say "no," ask if they mind if you bring a portable generator if you have one. If they say "no" to that, and you can't check any systems, keep that in mind when you make an offer.

There's no one perfect checklist for buying a classic or vintage camper. I use this list as a starting point and edit and expand as necessary for a particular camper. When you're getting serious about buying, take the time to research your specific type, model, and year in online owners forums or

A Spartan like this weighs in at just over 8,000 pounds, and it's over 40 feet long. If it's the direction you want to go, keep in mind the amount of commitment and cash you'll have to put into it (not to mention a big place to park it), depending on its condition. Just because it's cool doesn't mean it's "you."

Facebook groups. Buying a canvas pop-up camper is a lot different than a 40-foot Spartan, and each will have its own quirks and red flags.

Every specific possibility of good and bad qualities that a camper may have could take forever to list. But I will say that if a feature listed is important to you, and the seller says it works—especially if the price reflects a camper that has working systems—do everything you can to get them to let you try it out to ensure it actually does work. If they have added accessories or upgraded systems, ask who did the installation, and ask to see photos of the repairs before, during, and after. If they say the tires are almost new, check the manufacturers date. You'll learn how in the next chapter.

Aesthetics are important, but we also have to remain objective when inspecting a potential buy. Jess checks out a 1960s Mustang travel trailer that's intriguing and cool looking. It has since been purchased and renovated by someone whose boxes were all very happily checked.

The good sellers may still say that the previous owner said something works, and they are honest about what they know and don't know. The even better sellers have checked all the systems and can be honest about each item you are curious about. The best sellers show you what works and doesn't, and tells you to the best of their capability what needs to be done to make the camper roadworthy if it's not already. The best buyers do their research, look carefully all around the camper, and learn to listen to their gut and their nose. A trusty nose is a great buyer's tool. Some smells can be simply annoying, and many of them can be signs of must-fix problems. The smell of mold, for example, can't be eradicated without getting rid of the mold itself.

The sagginess in the front and/or rear of a camper means that there is structural damage. (AS)

Looking around the outside

First—do you like its look? It may be trivial to some, but make sure it looks like a camper you would actually use. Just because someone else said this was a good brand or model doesn't make it "you." There's no shame in wanting your camper to look a certain way.

Most older campers have wood for wall studs and framing. Check both the front and the rear of the camper where the camper meets the frame. If there are any buckles or wrinkles in the outer skin where they meet, then there is likely rot in those areas. When a camper's wooden frame rots, the skin loses its support and sags. Depending on the amount of rot, the frame and camper may not even be attached to one another in that area, and may signal the need for a total rebuild.

It's important to get a look under the camper. A little rust is to be expected due to age. But if there is a lot of rust, holes, cracks, bends, or large dents in the frame, it will need significant work or complete replacement.

Underneath

If you can see the frame, check it for bad rust. A little rust is to be expected due to age, and it can likely be treated. But if there are holes, breaks, or major dents in the frame, it will need significant work. If the jack is in good shape, raise the camper up a little and maybe you can see better. Note: Unless you're a pro and have the equipment to lift it safely, do not crawl under the camper—gingerly peek your head under, wear safety glasses, and be very careful.

If you can't see under the camper to look at the frame, reach underneath with your camera and take pictures where you can.

This shows the corrosion that occurs when aluminum sheeting is attached to a steel frame. It can be so bad that the aluminum is barely hanging on.

Depending on the camper, you may see a wooden frame all around the edges underneath, and you'll need to check its condition. If it is wet and soft, or dry and flaky, it is either rotten or on its way to being rotten. If you are planning a complete or partial rebuild, then this may not matter to you except to worry about it falling apart on the way home.

Some campers, like Airstreams, have belly pans attached under the frame so you may not be able to see if the frame is rusty. In that case, check what you can: look for corrosion around the rivets that attach the belly pan to the steel frame—this is very common because when steel and aluminum are in contact with one another, they have a chemical reaction that causes the aluminum to corrode, sometimes so much that the belly pan is hanging by a couple of rivets instead of being securely attached to the frame. You might be able to get a glance at the frame through one of these gaps. You can also see a couple of the frame outriggers in front of and in back of the wheels in the wheel well to give you an idea of the extent of rust.

Outside seams

Look closely at the camper's seams and trims. Are they screwed or riveted? Are the screws or rivets rusty? You'll probably want to remove the rusty ones and put in stainless steel ones, or aluminum rivets if it is riveted. Are there gobs of silicone caulking on the seams? That is probably an attempt to keep it from leaking—and maybe it works, but it's better to fix the area than to gob it up with caulk.

Are there areas where screws or rivets are missing? There could be a leak where the holes are.

Are there parts of the seam that are completely separated? If it's possible, pry the two parts apart carefully (very carefully, since it's not your camper yet) to see what's below—it might be rot or other forms of damage.

Outer skins

How do the outer skins look? Are they dented, or are there holes that need to be patched? A large dent could mean that there's some structural damage behind it. A hole means that water and critters could have been getting in.

If it's painted, how does the paint look? I've seen pristine paint jobs, and I've seen campers that have been covered sloppily in house paint with a cheap brush. The pristine one is much easier to deal with, but very rare unless it's a camper that has already been restored or renovated.

If the paint is flaking, bubbling, or just looks like crap, you'll likely want a new, improved paint job, whether you do it yourself or hire a pro painter.

Door, door latch, and lock

The door is the... well, door... to your safety and comfort. It's easy to tell if it basically works by opening and closing it, pulling on the door handle when it is closed to make sure it stays latched,

I always thought seam separation wouldn't be a big deal to fix until I actually had to try to fix it myself. We're talking potential major structural repairs.

and checking to make sure the hinges are tight. Is it in the right shape to conform to the body of the trailer? You should look around the door to see how well it is sealed. Most door gaskets are replaceable, but even the best gasket can't make a bent door leak proof.

Check the door handle to make sure that it isn't wobbly or broken, especially on the inside (besides getting in, you also need to get out!). If you have someone with you, one of you should go inside and lock the door, and the other should try to get in. How easy is it for the person inside to unlock it? If the lock works, does the seller have the key? In some cases that may not matter because the key cylinder can usually be swapped out. In other cases, though, you may have to search far and wide for a replacement handle and lock, and then pay a premium for it when you find it. I had to buy half an Airstream just to get a door and handle (story in a later chapter).

If the camper has a wooden frame and the door is sagging on its hinges, it could very well have rot in the door frame. If the door is saggy, then the door could be rotten.

Windows

Broken glass in a window is generally pretty obvious, so that's an easy item to judge—either it's broken or it's not. Take a look at each window from the outside and inside.

A broken window as a whole can be a straightforward fix, but if your camper has special windows that only that manufacturer made and used, then finding a replacement can take time and a good chunk of cash. For example, the curved windows on my Argosy can cost around $600 to $900 each—if you can find one. That's why I invested in a rock guard that is mounted over the windows to protect them going down the road. One set of OEM rockguards is cheaper than two broken curved windows. Many people make their own rock guards, or have a rockguard made to their specs.

Other campers have rockguards, too, so check to see if it has one—and if it does, how well it works. Are the arms broken, the material cracked? Does the mechanism to lock it in place work?

Check the handles to open and close the windows to make sure they are present and work properly. Some windows crank, some slide, and some have arms you lift that prop the window up.

Check the rubber gaskets around the windows. If it's missing, broken, or not flexible, you'll need to replace this in order to get a tight seal.

There should be some sort of aluminum drip guard or "eyebrow" over the top edge of the windows and door outside to divert water to the sides rather than into the window or door. There is often a rubber flap that slides into the window frame just above the window that may need to be replaced if it is no longer flexible.

Windows also shed light on water damage on the inside of a camper, especially if the inner walls are made of wood. A lot of sellers promise that there are no current leaks, but they might admit that

Painting over water damage without fixing the leak that caused it will force the paint to bubble, split, and peel.

at one point it had some. The trouble is, sometimes the damage is fixed but the *cause* of the damage still exists. Sometimes previous owners will have painted over water damage, so look for cracks and peeling in the paint. Push on the wood under a window to see if it is solid or "crunchy." If it moves and sounds crunchy, then there's likely water damage under there. If it's wet, that means that there's an active leak.

If the inner walls are a material other than wood, look for tell-tale water marks, like stains where there was once a drip, or where it may have pooled on the floor.

This is the water damage and mold often found under an old camper refrigerator.

Floors and ceiling

Those pooling places on the floor are another hint about where damage might be lurking. Wherever water may splash or drip on a regular basis, check for soft and/or 'crunchy' floors—under sinks, around a tub and toilet, under the refrigerator, and near the water inlet if there is one. On the ceiling, look for wetness, stains, and sagginess, all hints that there could be damage to the ceiling structure. Look closely around ceiling vents, fans, air conditioners, and other roof openings.

Unfortunately, there's a lot of gross stuff that can hide in the walls, like these rodent nests. The only way to assess the situation and then get rid of them is to open things up—which, of course, you can't do until after you buy. Your nose can tell you some of what might be hiding, since rodent urine and feces are stinky enough to smell from inside the walls.

Ooh, that smell

My absolute least favorite part of looking at an old camper is discovering its odors. You never know what it's going to smell like in there, no matter how old it is. If you're lucky, it will smell just a little stuffy since it has been closed up for a while. If it's typical, the camper you're surveying will sport a combination aura of mouse poop and pee, mold, mildew, and that weird "old foam" smell from the furniture. It could smell like smoke from a previous owner smoking in it, or like a litter box that the neighborhood cats have been frequenting.

If you fall in love with a camper that smells like [insert worst possible smelly thing here], you'll have to remember that it will take a lot of work to get rid of it. Some may be caused by surface issues (a mouse nest in a drawer, for example), or by embedded issues (mouse nests in the walls). The surface issues will be the easiest items to fix. If the old mattresses stink, getting rid of them and replacing them with new mattresses will solve part of the problem. But did the mattress have mold and/or mildew on the bottom side, or the side(s) against the wall? Is there apparent water damage over or near the bed? Are you willing to take on these problems?

Black mold, which can smell musty or like rotten vegetables, can grow anywhere that moisture collects—behind a tub surround, under a bed, in an old refrigerator, in insulation. Some of it is easy enough to find and clean out, since you can see and reach it. In Zola, I found black mold under the refrigerator, under the tub, and under the water tank—all places that happened to have leaks and subsequent wood rot. And all places that I couldn't reach without moving the refrigerator, tub, and water tank.

A whole lotta colors growing on this bathroom's surfaces. It was worse underneath the tub.

Pink mold—which technically is a bacteria, not a mold—is known to build up on shower walls, on shower curtains, under carpets, and behind wallpaper. Identifiable only by sight, it makes sense that it's tough to find and fight it if you can't see it.

Other smells are just gross, no matter what is causing them. I looked at an Argosy for sale a couple of years ago that the seller had listed for $900. It looked pretty good in the photos, so I made an appointment to look at it. I got there before the seller and walked around the outside. This is a good deal, I thought. When the seller arrived and let me inside, it was all I could do to go in the door. The smell inside was so intense and noxious that I was sure I'd find a bunch of dead, rotten somethings in there. Looking around it looked OK—no dead things. The most evident visible issue was a leak by the front window—not unusual for an Argosy. But that smell. I knew by then from experience that if a camper is gutted, you're much more likely to be able to get rid of the unwanted smells because you're getting rid of the unwanted sources of the smells. And once it's gutted and you seal up leaks and holes where critters get in, you'll help to prevent smells from coming back.

But I couldn't take it. I thought maybe I could buy it and part it out, but I couldn't stand the thought of going into that camper again, or bringing home whatever was in there.

I've seen this very same camper come up for sale a couple of times for $2,400, and it makes me wonder if the new seller really put in $1,500 worth of fixes into it. Part of me is tempted to go take a look at it to see if they got rid of that horrendous odor because it would probably be worth the price even if it's just used for parts. But I can't bring myself to find out.

9

GETTING HOME SAFELY & LEGALLY

THE LEGAL DEFINITION of "road-worthy" varies state by state, but there are some basics that are necessary for safety no matter where you're traveling. Towing with an appropriate vehicle, making sure the tires and rims are sound, and being prepared to check lights are all keys to your safety. And you should be prepared for things to go wrong. One piece of practical advice: Just because your vehicle is rated to pull, say, 3,000 pounds, it does not mean that you *should* tow 3,000 pounds. Your

My choice for a tow vehicle has to include a large gas tank so I don't have to stop for fuel as often as with a standard tank, a backup camera to help with hitching up, and a towing package that has more capacity than I need just to be safe.

best resource is your dealer, your mechanic, and professional opinions on what vehicles will work and how they should be set up to do so.

If you take sadistic pleasure in kicking off a heated debate in any camper group or forum, start asking about tow vehicles. Once you weed out and ignore any annoying comments, you're probably going to find at least a couple of other people that are willing to share their experience with towing with the same brand and model vehicle you are thinking of towing with.

My truck is rated to tow up to 12,200 pounds. I haven't towed anything that weighs that much, but it's not really something I want to try. If I had to pull something approaching that weight, I would want to have a more powerful tow vehicle.. The average camper weighs a little over 5,000

BEFORE YOU BUY A VINTAGE CAMPER

I added clamp-on towing mirrors for increased visibility behind me.

pounds empty (sometimes referred to as 'dry weight' or 'curb weight') although many smaller vintage and classic campers weigh a lot less. My two Airstream Argosys are 2,800 and 4,100 pounds respectively, with Gross Vehicle Weight Ratings (GVWR) of 4,450 and 6,200 pounds—the recommended maximum weight the camper and its cargo can weigh to be towed safely. The weight of propane, water, clothes, food, and other items you plan to bring along with you need to be considered when making your choice.

Besides towing capability, think about what other attributes you want in your vehicle. For example, a backup camera and a GPS. One of my favorite features in my truck is its extended range 36-gallon gas tank. Having a tank that size means I don't have to stop for gas as often as I would with a standard 23 to 26-gallon tank. Another favorite thing about the two tow vehicles I've had: Both

Check to make sure it the hitch receiver solidly bolted or welded on. Look for a sticker, like this one on the right, that states what trailer and tongue weights it is rated for.

were used and had low mileage, so that saved me a significant amount of money for a truck that was in excellent condition.

Tow mirrors

With a standard camper hitched up behind you, you lose the ability to use your rear-view mirror. If your vehicle has side mirrors that don't protrude very far, you may want to get a pair of clamp-on towing mirrors that extend the range of what you can see. Your mirrors should be visible from behind the camper. This is critical for seeing traffic behind you.

If you plan to travel on toll roads, it's important to have a driver-side mirror that folds tight against the side of your vehicle to be able to get close to the toll booth without hitting anything.

BEFORE YOU BUY A VINTAGE CAMPER

Safety chains are necessary to keep the camper hitch from hitting the ground and to keep the camper attached to your vehicle if the hitch fails. Note the brass-colored coupler pin, which keeps the locking lever in place.(AS)

A good connection

Check the hitch receiver to make sure it is solidly bolted or welded on, and that it is rated for pulling what you need to pull. You do not want the camper to fly away from your vehicle if a hitch breaks or detaches. Check the locking lever on the trailer to make sure it opens and closes cleanly. Ideally the locking lever on the coupler will have a way to be secured so that it doesn't pop up while driving. A trailer coupler pin generally ranges from $1 to $20, a fair price for piece of mind. If I'm on a long trip, I'll use a padlock as my coupler pin to slow down anyone who might be thinking of trying to haul my camper away when I'm not looking.

The tire date code is to the right of the letters DOT, in the last oval. The numbers 4318 stamped into it tells us this tire was made in the 43rd week of 2018.

Safety chains

Do not tow even a little way without making sure there are safety chains on the camper. Safety chains are just that: added safety in case the hitch disengages. Thankfully, the one time I was buying a camper that didn't have safety chains, the seller offered to have them welded on later that day. If the owner is not willing to do this, you may have to weld them on yourself (if you know how and have the equipment with you) or contact a local welder to come out to the site to weld them on.

You can see the break in the ring around the rim on the left.

Solid tires

Tires made after 2000 have a tire date code stamped on them, so if the seller states that they put on new tires, you can confirm the tire age by figuring out when they were made. This is important since many tire manufacturers recommend tire replacement every 10 years whether you've used them or not. A tire can have all kinds of words, letters, and numbers stamped on them. The tire date code is in the same line as the letters DOT, to the right, in the last oval.

Even if the tires are less than 10 years old, if the tires are bald, flat, dry, and/or cracked, they should be replaced.

Safe rims

Is the camper you're looking at a 1968 or older? If so, check for split rims. These rims are nicknamed 'suicide rims' or 'widow makers'. Now illegal, split rims are made of two or more parts and are susceptible to forcefully flying apart when the tire is being filled up with air or when a tire is mounted. A split rim is identifiable by a break in the ring. That ring is prone to flying off and injuring or killing a person it its path. DO NOT EVER try to take the tires off of the split rim yourself. It's not worth dying over.

If the camper has wheels with split rims, it is always recommended that a camper be trailered rather than towed. I've only towed one camper that had split rims, and I went about 20 miles very slowly and I was nervous the whole time. When I sold it, I told potential buyers that they had to put new wheels and tires on it or put it on a trailer to take it home.

Title and bill of sale

I'm going to tell you both the most common question ever asked about titles, and the most common answer to that question. They are both easy to remember.

Q: Can I register my camper without a title?

A: It depends on your state and its rules.

In other words, there's no hard-and-fast national rule about titles, so you're on your own in finding out what your state needs from you in order to register an old camper. Check with your state department of motor vehicles. Vermont, for example, has a rule that if a vehicle is more than 15 years old, it does not require a title to be registered, only a bill of sale (as of this writing). Vermont also will not issue titles for trailers that have an empty weight of 1,500 pounds or less.

License plate or permit

While you're on the phone with the DMV, ask what the law is in your state for towing a camper home from a seller, especially if you are going to be crossing state lines. Some states require special

If your lights stop working, memorize these old-school hand signals used to properly signal your intent to turn and stop to other drivers. (AS)

temporary moving permits, some want the camper to be fully registered and insured. Some might have very lenient requirements, but it would be terrible to find that out the hard way.

Signal and brake lights

To safely and legally haul a trailer, you'll want it to have working signal and brake lights. You'll find out if the ones on the camper work when you plug the camper's 4-pin or 7-pin power cord to your vehicle.

Even if a seller tells me that the lights work, I always carry a magnetic towing light kit when I pick up a camper. Depending on the model of the towing lights, it will have a four or seven pin plug to attach to your vehicle, and then a 20-foot or so length of wire with two red signal/brake lights that magnetically attach to your camper's rear bumper. Extensions are available if your camper is longer.

Now you have working, legal signal and brake lights. The only issue I've had with these kinds of lights is when the rear of my camper doesn't have any accessible steel for the magnets to attach to. I brought my 28-foot Argosy home from Michigan with the lights duct-taped on to its aluminum bumper. Not pretty, but they worked.

Above you'll see hand signals that can make you legal in a pinch. These signals conform to the Uniform Vehicle Code that all state laws observe, and you probably learned them in your driver's ed class, remember?

Sway bars and weight distribution bars

You may not be able to install a sway bar for your trip home unless you bring along the equipment to mount the sway control ball, but you should be able to install a weight distribution kit on your camper for the trip home since you can install it with that adjustable wrench you have tucked away in your glove compartment. As their names suggest, sway bars help prevent your trailer from swaying back and forth, and weight distribution bars help to distribute the trailer tongue weight from one point (the hitch ball) to both axles of the tow vehicle for better overall control.

You can also do some common sense checking of the travel trailer before you set out to help prevent sway. For example, in both of my Argosys, much of the interior had been taken out because the previous owner had planned to make changes. When I bought them, they sellers put all the parts and pieces back in, stacked up rather than put back where they were originally. What this meant was that most of the weight in the camper was toward the back rather than over the axles and forward of the axles. A quick solution is to offer to help them put the stuff in, so you can have control of the lighter items in the back and the heavier items closer to the front. Watch this video on YouTube (I made a short link so it is easier to copy) to see why: **cutt.ly/sway**.

10

MAKING CHANGES

I'VE OFTEN OVERHEARD DISCUSSIONS—some quite heated—in vintage-camper groups about whether or not an owner should keep their camper's original layout and design, or completely redo it to make it modern. Most people, I think, shoot for something comfortably in between those two things. Before I get into the topic of restoration versus renovation versus remodeling and so on,

One of the many painstakingly restored campers on display at the RV/MH Hall of Fame in Elkhart, Indiana.

I want to clarify that I believe that you can do whatever you want to your camper since you paid for it fair and square. It's your camper, so it's your decision(s).

Just because it's your decision doesn't mean it's an easy one, though. You should take time to consider whether or not you want to keep the camper as original as possible and restore its function, or if you want to redo and remake the camper to reflect your unique ideas and personality. If you're not sure what you want to do, and your camper is healthy and safe enough to camp in, leave it as is and see how you like it, and take note of things that you wish were different. Scour Pinterest for new layout ideas. Change what you want and leave the rest as is.

What you ultimately decide will depend on several factors: Your skill, budget, motivation, the current shape of the camper, your dreams, and your plans.

A beautifully renovated travel trailer. (AS)

Restoring a vintage or classic camper is the art of putting a trailer back together in its original form with original parts (if possible) or precise, era-appropriate reproduction parts. Just like with anything antique or vintage, it can take a lot of research, time, money, and skill to restore a camper to its original glory, especially if it is particularly rare or old. Finding original gas lights and intact working iceboxes, for example, are much harder to find than a modern LED camper light and travel-trailer mini-fridge.

Hiring experts (or becoming an expert) in vintage camper restoration takes time, money, and time and money. Did I mention it takes time and money? It does. It also requires a dedication to studying the history of a camper to understand why it works and looks the way it does. It's critical to know how to determine if original systems are safe to re-use and which were pulled off the mar-

Jess replacing her original beat up teardrop marker lights with LED reproductions from Vintage Trailer Supply. [vintagetrailersupply.com]

ket due to safety issues. Knowing the history of a particular camper will reveal any quirks that the original design had so that you can avoid, remove, or improve them if you want to.

True restoration revives a historical piece, able to be used in the same way as intended when first created. A museum piece may not need to have a working systems, but a camper trailer meant to be used will have original features in working order. If you're seeking to make your camper into a collector's item, this is the direction you'll be heading.

Removing a non-working original fan in preparation of installing a new moder one.

Repair and Replace

A somewhat self-explanatory category, repair of a camper is just that: Fixing what is broken so it can be livable and get back on the road. Wood is rotten so you replace the wood. The roof leaks so you fix the roof. A tire keeps going flat so you replace the tire. Nearly all of us will be repairing and re-placing something to make a camper safe to use and pull.

The key word in this section is 'repair'. A repair is not the same as a makeshift temporary fix to get you and your camper home, or a layer of paint to cover up water stains. A repair is a dedicated fix to the problem—fixing the water leak in this case—not a temporary cover-up.

A new roof fan replaces the original fan without taking away from the original travel-trailer vibe.

Renovation

Renovating is where restoration and modernization meet. The goal is usually to keep the camper as original in design as possible, while adding modern features and technology. A challenge is hiding the new stuff so it won't take away from any of the camper's vintage/original appeal. Some obvious examples may be replacing all old wiring with new and safer wiring, replacing an axle for a smoother and safer ride, replacing an icebox with a modern fridge, replacing dangerous split rims and tires with safe rims and tires, incorporating a new furnace, cooling system, stove, hot water heater, or fridge, adding or replacing waste tanks, switching out incandescent lights for LED, adding a solar power system, and so on.

BEFORE YOU BUY A VINTAGE CAMPER

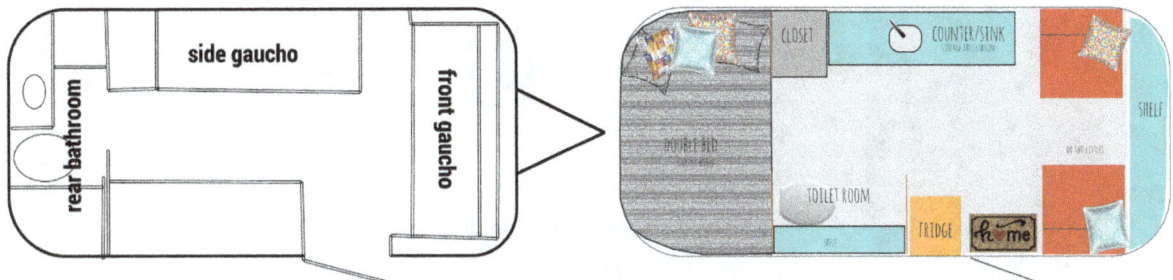

On the left is my Argosy 20's original layout. There was a bunk over the side gaucho. The sink, stove, and fridge were on the opposite side (curb side) of the trailer. On the right is one my drawing that represents how the interior was remodeled during its rebuild.

Remodeling

When remodeling a camper, you're basically taking it apart and putting it back together the way that you want it to be. This is what I did with Zola. She originally had a gaucho couch in the front that pulled out into a full-size bed, then a gaucho couch on the side that pulled out into a full-size bed, and then a bunk over the side bed. How five people would get along in a 16' by 8' space is difficult to imagine—almost as difficult as having to get to the bathroom in the rear from the front bed when the side bed was taking up the entire walkway. I didn't need to sleep five and I didn't want to crawl over a bed to go to the bathroom, so I decided to rearrange the layout roughly based on a current 19-foot Airstream model. I wanted the bed in the back, toilet on the side, kitchen on the opposite side, and chairs/table in the front. I decided against a furnace, oven, shower, and hot water heater. Instead of a flush toilet, I wanted to use a composting toilet because I didn't want to deal with a black tank. I didn't want to install anything that ran on propane because I wasn't so sure of my abilities with it. Now I know that I could hire someone to plumb and connect propane safely if I choose to go that route.

Affecting value

Die-hard restorers have been known to scoff at or even scold those of us who decide to change our vintage and classic campers drastically. In their defense, it generally does increase the value of a vin-

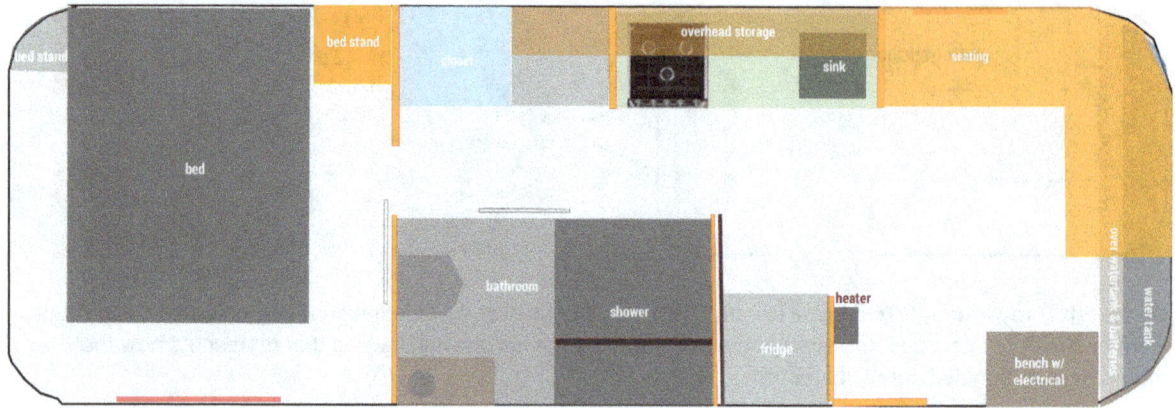

My choice with Zack is to rebuild it to have the original layout with a few changes to accomodate updated appliances and systems.

tage camper to repair and restore the insides by following the plan of the original designers. Many of the insides of these campers are walled and ceilinged with stained and varnished wood paneling that emphasizes cool patterns and depth in the wood. It's absolutely beautiful.

Still, many people decide to paint over their original wood—usually in a shade of white—to make the inside of a small camper seem bigger and lighter. I may be wrong, but I'd bet that this is the number one area of contention among restorers and renovators—if you don't agree, join a vintage restoring group and ask them if they think you should paint the inside of your vintage camper. The most passionate of the naysayers may give you some not-so-friendly suggestions of where to stick your paint. The more humane purists will let you know why it's not a good idea in their opinion (historical value, resale value, etc.), and they hope you'll keep it original, but will also agree that it's your camper and your decision.

Next steps

Whatever direction you choose to take, and whether you think you want to take on the work yourself or hire a professional, take time to give it a healthy amount of thought. I know for me, taking that time isn't that easy because I like a project best when it's done. But I do make drawings, like the one above, and I recommend that whether or not you are artistically inclined, make drawings to compare different layouts. Look up old brochures to see if there are photos or sketches of your trailer in its brand new condition. Spend some time going through *Vintage Camper Trailer Magazine* and *Vintage Trailer Magazine*, and books in the Resources chapter. Join groups like Vintage Trailer Restoration, Restoring Vintage Trailers, or Airstream Restoration on Facebook (and join clubs in person when it is safe to do so) and ask others to share photos of their camper layouts and let you know why they decided to do what they did—many people in these groups absolutely love to show off their camper and share their ideas.

CRYSTAL MCCULLOUGH

Dawkins and Lexie inspecting Zola's updates.

11

LIPSTICK, SCAMS, & POLISHED TURDS

HAVE YOU HEARD the terms 'lipstick on a pig' or 'polished turd'? Neither one conjures up an appetizing visual, and there's a reason for that. Both terms refer to campers that have had aesthetic tweaks that may make it look better. These tweaks, however, hide defects or even dangerous structural issues—sometimes on purpose, sometimes not. The term 'polished turd' is generally used to

That little harmless-looking sag on the left above the bumper is a sign that there is likely structural damage to the camper's frame.

describe a deceptively polished Airstream. A gorgeously shiny Airstream is a beauty to behold, and sometimes a buyer can be blinded by its twinkly splendor and miss the non-pretty issues.

A summer or two ago, camper owner and my now-friend Maggie reached out in a Facebook group to ask if anyone in the New England area would help her install wiring and a solar panel on her vintage Road Runner. No one replied to her, and she said all pros she contacted in the area were booked up, so I reached out and told her I would be happy to do what I could for her. She had driven her little 1971 Road Runner camper to New England from Kansas, so she didn't have far to bring her camper here.

BEFORE YOU BUY A VINTAGE CAMPER

When she got here with her camper, I could see clearly just how much she loved it. She had spent a couple thousand to buy it, and had recently paid a carpenter several thousand dollars to replace the rear inner paneling, and repair and build cabinets. She asked that besides the wiring for solar, if I would give her a quote for replacing the outside corner trim since there were dents in it. It's a straightforward project, and I said I would take a look and give her an estimate for the work.

A sample of the frame on the left rear corner of the Road Runner.

The Road Runner was a cute little thing, with seafoam green and silver paint on the outside, and beautifully decorated on the inside. The walls and cabinet were gorgeous stained wood and looked great. Maggie left it here for me to work on and planned to be back in a couple of months to pick it up.

Once I got to work on it, I noticed the aluminum was sagging a bit over the frame in the rear and there were a couple of places where the aluminum was wavy. I had to take the trim off anyway, and when I did that, the screws holding it were not resisting, which told me that there was rot in the wood. I removed the trim with the intention of also removing the lower back panel to get a better look at what was going on. There were several areas where the panels were no longer attached to one another.

| 121 |

As I removed the rear bottom aluminum sheet, chunks of rotten wood fell to the ground. There was nothing—literally nothing—that was structurally sound in the rear of that camper. Maggie had to have had a really diligent guardian angel to have made it this far without the thing collapsing.

It was heartbreaking to have to call her and tell her what I found. She told me that her carpenter had told her that he found absolutely no rot. Of course, this was impossible, since he had seen the exact same rotten supports that I did not long ago—the only difference was that he saw them from the inside. She was upset, but asked if I could replace the rotted wood and I told her I'd look at the camper further to get the full scope of the problem and let her know what I could do. Sadly, I found that wood had rotted most of the way around the frame and almost all the way up the sides—meaning the camper was barely attached to itself. Which, in turn, meant it needed a total rebuild. This is not what either of us expected, but there was no way around it—there's not really any 'sorta' fixing a camper's structure, and it's not in my nature to lie about what needs to be done and just cover it up. I'd never done that amount of work for anyone, so I talked to a couple of expert restorers/renovators to find out about their schedules and what their going rate is for a rebuild. When I told her that it could

The wood frame all around the Road Runner was rotten, so nails, staples, and screws had nothing solid to attach to. You can see some of the pieces of wood falling out after I removed the first exterior aluminum panel. Note the new panelling the previous "pro" had put in. He told the camper owner that the camper had no rot.

be anywhere from $1,200 to $2,500 a foot for labor and materials—or $14,400 to $30,000—let's just say that she wasn't very happy.

I wasn't happy either. It's safe to assume that there are a few camper sellers out there that don't know what's wrong with their camper, so they sell it with good intent even if it's not as sound as they thought. Annoying, and maybe expensive, but they weren't trying to rip anyone off. But a person calling themselves a "professional" carpenter or renovator—or even a non-professional carpenter or renovator—knows that you don't build something on or over rotten wood that is falling apart in chunks and then tell the client you didn't see it. And yet, obviously, it happens. And it happens way too much. Maggie had trusted her seller and her carpenter (and why shouldn't she?), only to be left with beautiful and expensive lipstick covering a camper that was in danger of disintegrating any minute if she'd kept going as is.

Maggie decided to sell her Road Runner, and sadly, couldn't ask more than a few hundred dollars for it. She was honest in her for-sale listing, and open with the potential buyers about the need for a full rebuild.

Avoiding scams

Travel-trailer sales listings are not immune to scams, and it's important to take the time to learn some of the red flags. This screenshot shows a small percentage of Facebook listings I found just this morning when searching for *camper*.

- Super-low prices on typically expensive travel trailers, like newer Airstreams or Scamps;
- mentions of random features not found on campers, like 'sun roof' or 'automatic transmission';
- listings usually have only one photo available;
- seller profile might have zero to a handful of followers or claims to be a dealership;
- the join date shows that the seller has only recently joined Facebook;

- scammer uses the same photo in different geographical areas;
- bizarre VIN numbers—sometimes using the same fake VIN on different listings or different VINs for the same camper;
- wording is grammatically questionable;
- seller will try to get you to communicate via direct email or text rather than the Craigslist or Facebook communication methods;
- description as a whole is totally random, like the photo is a Casita trailer and the description is of a computer or lawnmower.

If you contact the so-called seller, they often use a variation of common counterfeit explanations for their odd pricing and listings: "…it's so cheap because I need to get rid of it quickly. My husband/wife died and it brings back too many memories… I'd send more pics but I'm in Texas in the military about to be deployed to _____ and the camper is in Colorado… if you send me $$$ I'll have it shipped to you…" etc., etc.

To report a listing in Facebook Marketplace, click on the three dots … and choose Report Post. I also report the seller. On Craigslist, click on the flag icon to mark it for review. It doesn't stop scams from happening, but hopefully it helps a few people to avoid getting taken.

The pros—who can we trust?

Ever since I worked on my first travel trailer, people have told me, "Crystal, you should become a professional renovator/restorer!" As flattering as this may be—and with all due respect—these people do not know what they are talking about.

I've worked on a variety of renovation elements, but I don't have the experience necessary to become a pro travel-trailer restorer or renovator, nor do I have the equipment, space, funds, or professional team available to do it properly. The part of travel trailer renovation and restoration in which I feel I've reached expert status is in persisting to learn as much as I can and to do my best in communicating to others what I've learned. I've been an instructor and an author for many years, so the how-to sharing-my-experience thing makes a lot more practical and logical sense for me.

BEFORE YOU BUY A VINTAGE CAMPER

We live in a time when an article in *Dwell*, *Apartment Therapy*, or a viral post on Instagram can turn a one-camper-fixer into a star. They'll have people contacting them from all over to do to their campers what they did for their own. Who wouldn't want to make beautiful campers all the time? And so businesses are born, and both parties are thrust into uncharted territory, hoping things will work out. For lack of another term, I call these *the new pros*.

How do we know who to trust and who not to? Is popularity the way to judge quality work? Every pro has to start somewhere, right? There have been some great success stories of people turning pro after fixing up one or two campers and getting media coverage for their work. The long-term successes usually have some relevant experience, such as construction/cabinet-making or an autobody background that can be adapted and applied to camper rebuilding. They show willingness to admit they don't know everything and hire others who can do what they can't. They show both the shiny filtered Instagram pics and the rusty sweaty ones; they share problems they run into, and solutions they find. If they hire a subcontractor, they accept responsibility for the subcontractor's work.

We live in a time when a beautiful set of photos on Instagram can bring fame to a one-time camper renovator/redecorator.

Asking around is one way to find information about a pro. Ask about the ones that have been in business for a while, too. Looking at their portfolio of work—in person, if possible—is one way to get an idea of what they are capable of. Find out what kind of team they have, and what their skill sets are. Use what you learned in this book and in your research to see if they are a match for you. For example, I tend to pay attention to things like whether they tend to only replace original fridges with one of the new retro-influenced

Experiences like Maggie's are heartbreaking and expensive. We can never avoid all problems all the time, but hopefully we can avoid this.

mini fridges, and include a space heater or an electric fireplace heater rather than including a choice of updating your wiring and propane to power an RV refrigerator and furnace.

I'm not a mini fridge/space heater snob. I have put mini fridges and space heaters in campers, including Zola when I use her as a rental. These cute retro mini-fridges are cost and energy efficient, are usually easy to find, and come in many colors. Those renting Zola aren't going far and will be plugged in the whole time they are at a campsite. 110 mini fridges cost significantly less than a refrigerator designed for travel trailer/RV use, and space heaters are easier to install than a propane furnace. They are great for camping with hookups, when you are plugged into shore power or a generator.

While this may all seem obvious, repetitive, and perhaps superfluous, I really, really, really want anyone you hire to give you what you want and need specifically for you within your budget—whether for a full overhaul, a leak repair, or a paint job. It's heartbreaking to hear stories of people who lose deposits and end up with an unfinished or ruined travel trailer because who they hired couldn't do the work.

I asked fellow classic and vintage camper owners how they vet a renovator/restorer: A pro should be able to tell you *no* as well as *yes*—that what you want isn't recommended, or maybe it's beyond their current skill level or their schedule won't allow them to finish within your desired timeframe. They should know that a traveling camper has to keep weight and weight distribution in mind, and only parked ones should go wild with tile and hardwood. They should know how travel trailers are constructed and rules of structural integrity. They should be honest with you about how much time and money it will take, and not ghost you when you try to reach them to ask what the status in. Like sales scams, their price shouldn't be unrealistic compared to others in the field. They should have photos of not just finished travel trailer projects, but snapshots before and during the progress during their projects. If they get offended and can't come up with references or logs of their work, it's a good sign to look elsewhere. I agree with those that say the pro's professionalism, transparency, and level of respect for customers are necessary requirements, as well.

The moral of this chapter is that as tempting as it may be, we shouldn't buy based only on a camper's aesthetics, and we should only consider a self-proclaimed camper renovator/restorer if they have multiple positive references that can be verified. This doesn't mean that we can't trust anyone ever, although sometimes it's tempting. It means that there are specific things to look out for and red flags that shouldn't be ignored. We can't stop someone from ripping us off, but we are responsible for doing our homework. And now I'll stop being bossy.

CRYSTAL MCCULLOUGH

A well-restored 1961 Shasta.

12

PARTS, TOOLS, & OTHER COSTS

WHEN I MADE THE COMMITMENT to charge forward into Zola's rebuild and remodel myself, I thought I'd take care of what I believed to be a couple of the most direct and simple fixes and I'd be halfway done. I needed to find and replace the door handle and get a screen door. I mean, how hard can it be to find a door handle for a camper?

Let me answer that for you now that I know.

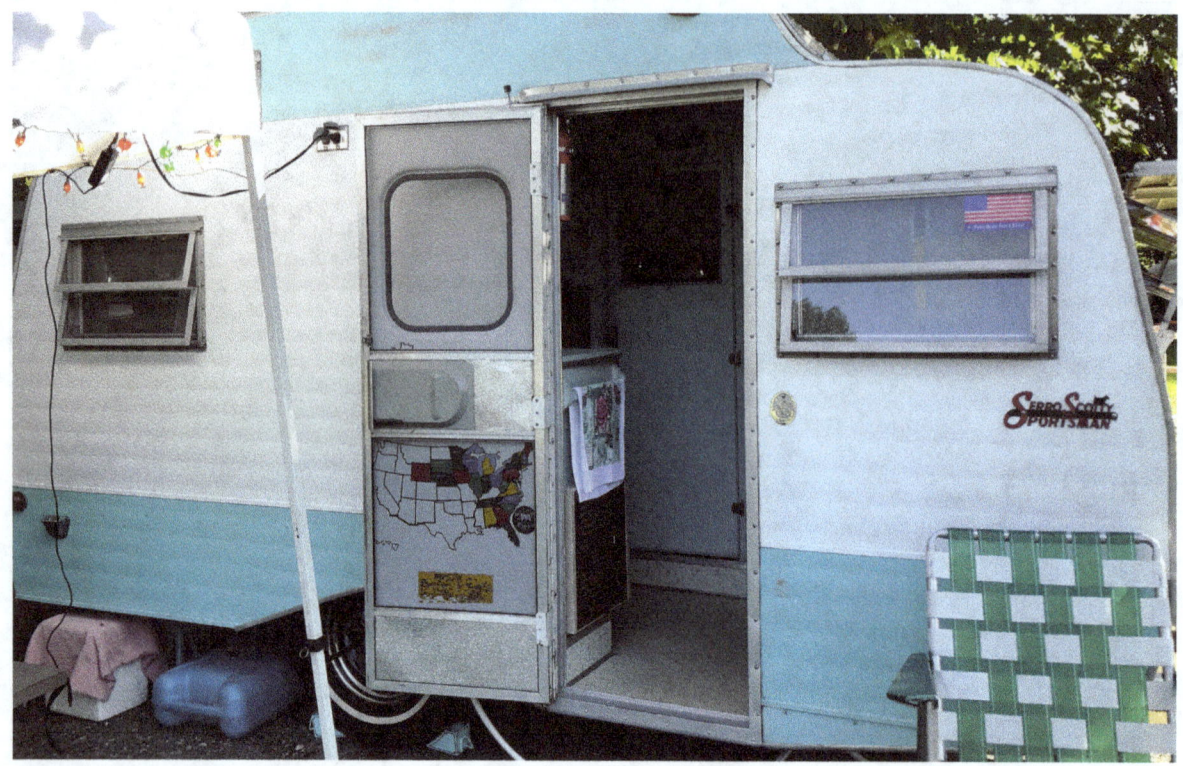

Suicide doors are those that have the handle toward the front of the camper and hinges toward the back. If not secured well, they can fly open while driving and cause some major damage to the door and camper.

Backstory: Some campers are designed with a suicide entrance door. What this means: As you face the door with the hitch to your right, the hinges are on the left side side of the door and the handle is on the right side of the door, toward the front. The designers did this, presumably, to keep the door from knocking into the awning arm when the door swung open. While the awning arm stayed safe in this arrangement, what often happened was far worse: As the trailer is being pulled down the road at 55+ miles per hour, the wind can catch the edge of the door and force it open, slamming the door into the side of the camper causing damage to the door, the camper, and your ego.

Given its dents and its out-of-whack door frame, it was clear that this mishap occurred at least one time to Zola. There's a gouge on her side right next to the door, so it's also possible a previ-

Damage is obvious around the door to the small Argosy. To start, there are deep dents by the hinges and a gouge in the door trim near the bottom right area of the door. I didn't realize the original door had been replaced until the color difference and atypical handle were pointed out to me.

ous owner caught the door on something while driving, and yanked and/or slammed the door hard enough to both ruin the door and alter the angle of the door frame.

Even though it was obvious my door was a slightly different color than the body of the camper, it wasn't until I started looking for a replacement door handle that it was pointed out to me that my Airstream Argosy door and handle were not original.

I found out later by a previous-previous owner that this different-looking door was built by an airplane repair person out of sheet steel (the original door was aluminum). The steel replacement door worked, but it was also heavy enough to require a hearty combination of lift and shove to get the door closed. No biggie, I thought, this will be an easy fix. Just buy a new door.

It's hard to believe this old beat-up door handle is worth hundreds of dollars.

Realization hit quickly: Used doors were really hard to find. Maybe the fact that it had a homemade steel door should have been a hint that this would be the case. The couple of times I found one for sale, they were priced around $900 or too far away to be picked up. Shipping would be exorbitant. Used screen doors were an additional several hundred dollars. Door handles in various conditions were selling from $300 to $700 or so.

I decided that I'd find a replacement handle for the current door and live with it; I figured closing the door would count as a workout (this was before I knew about trying to keep weight equal on the two sides of the trailer). I found a complete used handle without keys and replaced the broken one following directions I found in a YouTube video.

In the meantime, up popped a 22-foot 1972 Argosy for sale for $1,200, located about three hours away. It wasn't in great shape, but the photos showed it included my holy grail: An original working door handle on a non-damaged door—with the added bonus of a working screen door. On a whim, I called my sister Lois and brother-in-law Russell and asked if they wanted to go look at it with me. After looking it over, we asked the seller if he'd mind that we go have lunch and think it over. During lunch, the three of us discussed going in together on the camper: I would pay half of the price of the camper if I could have the doors and handle, and they would get the camper plus my current door with its new handle. A few hours later, we had paid $900 for the whole thing, and they got a new-to-them 22-foot Argosy for $450 (before you feel sorry for them for getting an Argosy with a crappy door, go back and read about their unicorn in chapter 7).

The bonus screen door that came with my new door and handle from the donor camper.

With my sister Diane's help, I removed Lois's door. I struggled getting my steel door off on my own. I knew it was heavier than the stock door, but I didn't realize just how heavy until it fell to the ground and I couldn't move it. When Dwayne got home, he picked up the door and loaded it in my truck. He estimated that it weighed well over 100 pounds.

Once it was off, I installed the new door, and did my best to line everything up.

Reading this, it might seem like the door replacement took about two to four days. When I go back and look at notes and photos, I can see that I bought that extra Argosy with Lois and Russell in late May, 2017, and I did the door swap in late October, 2017. I did my best to try to adjust the new door to the correct curve of my Airstream using turnbuckles and sheer force over the winter (based on suggestions from other owners), but I finally had to hire a professional Airstream restorer to fit my door properly and get the deadbolt to work—that was taken care of in September, 2018.

My costs for the replacement door and handle were better than buying a brand new door or having one custom manufactured, but it still wasn't cheap:

first replacement handle	$100
"new" door, handle, & screen door	$450
new hinges	$200
nuts/bolts	$7
new door seal	$30
deadbolt	$60
professional door fix	$800
TOTAL	**$1,647**

Thankfully, there are sources for original and reproduction parts and pieces for a lot of different old campers. Top of mind is Vintage Trailer Supply out of New Mexico—an online store that was recommended and used by me many times to find lights, knobs, gaskets, fixtures, and so on. Other online stores I've used are Out of Doors Mart, Inland RV, and Airstream Supply. My first replacement handle was purchased from an eBay seller, and I found an original used Airstream access door that I added to the back of the camper for a fair price there, too.

Other camper owners were one of my best sources. I've purchased leftover bolts at a discount from another DIY renovator—he could only find them in bulk and only needed a handful, and I bought his leftovers. I've purchased banana wraps, screen door protectors, and more from other owners in forums and Facebook Marketplace.

Some of these are tools I never thought I'd use, like chisels, the metal grinder, a Dremel oscillating tool, and a heat gun. It turns out I use them all the time.

I bought wiring, nuts and bolts, subflooring, and insulation from local hardware and lumber stores. I bought aluminum from a family owned airplane-materials store called Airparts Inc., based in Kansas. [airparts.com] I used Amazon when I couldn't find items anywhere else.

Unfortunately, some products go out of stock fast, and some are very expensive. I never would have imagined that a door handle for my camper would cost hundreds of dollars, nor did I ever think I'd go halvsies on an entire camper to get its door. Some products are things I never would have ever noticed or missed except that they were... well, missing... like the fuzzy stuff that keeps bugs out that is glued to the screen slots in which the window support arms go up and down. Someone somewhere manufactures that, thankfully, and someone sells it to us.

Nuts, bolts, rivets, light bulbs, wire, plugs, outlets, insulation, knobs, cleaning materials, vulkem caulking, butyl tape, trims, metal prep and rust prevention materials, flooring, locks, curtain tabs, toilet, bedding, paint, paint stripper, fan, appliances, rungs, a new axle—the stuff really adds up fast.

Tools are needed to remove and install all of the previous items: a pneumatic rivet gun and air compressor, hand riveter, Olympic rivet shaver, buck riveter kit, metal snippers, scrapers, paint brushes, paint rollers (or sprayer if you go that route), pressure washer, drill, various saws, bits, blades, oscillating tool, rotary metal cutter, sander, ladders—I could go on and on. Thankfully, I have a contractor husband I can borrow some items and expertise from. But he has to use his stuff, too, so I don't always have his tools immediately available.

Random cost examples

When I first decided to replace Zola's old insulation, questions and searches for information steered me away from the pink fiberglass stuff since it is a favorite housing for mice, and it holds water, which invites mold and mildew to grow. I decided to go with Rockwool [rockwool.com] insulation that is made from stone that has been melted and spun into fibers much like cotton candy is spun. Note: Owens Corning, the "pink stuff" insulation manufacturer, also makes a stone wool insulation dubbed Thermafiber. [owenscorning.com]

I used rock wool insulation in my 20-footer (shown here), and sheep's wool insulation in the 28-footer.

An insulation popular in the van-life community is sheep's wool insulation, and I'm seeing more camper renovators using it these days, too—I'm using it in my 28' Argosy. A few brands include Havelock Wool [havelockwool.com], Black Mountain Sheep Wool [blackmountaininsulation.com], and Oregon Shepherd [oregonshepherd.com].

Current prices for insulation covering one square foot (note: I sliced the 3.5" Rockwool in half to better fit my campers' 1.5" wallspace, so my cost was approximately 40.5 cents per square foot):

Havelock wool batting	2" thick	$1.20
Rockwool batting	3.5" thick	$.81
Rockwool rigid board	2" thick	$1.42
Pink Eco Touch fiberglass	2.5" thick	$.26

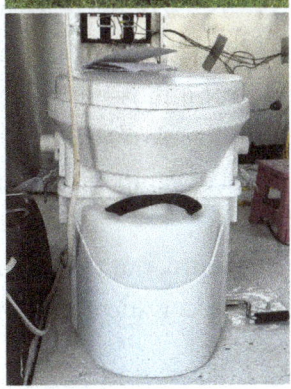

A standard portable camping toilet and a Nature's Head composting toilet. Their price points are hundreds of dollars apart.

Let's say you're thinking of replacing and/or installing a camper toilet. There are a range of options there, too. There are cassette toilets that store waste in a bottom section of the toilet itself. To empty it, you have to remove the cassette and dump it in your house toilet or at a dumping station. These toilets are often portable so you can use them no matter where you are camping (tent, camper, van). Portable cassette toilets cost roughly $70 to $150.

There are camper toilets similar to home toilets that flush into a holding tank. They cost from about $100 to $650. If you need to add or replace a waste tank, that will cost around $150 to $600 depending on size.

Composting toilets can cost around $400 up to $1,700. The two most popular brands are Nature's Head and Air Head toilets, both costing around $1,000. They are great for boondocking and stay smell-free because they divert liquid waste from solid waste. If you'd rather not spend $1K and you want to go the compost route, there are several resources online for directions on how to make your own less-costly composting toilet. [natureshead.net and airheadtoilet.com]

Next time I'm putting together a camper to rent either as an Airbnb or through Outdoorsy, my plan is to add a Laveo Dry Flush toilet. [dryflush.com] As the name implies, it doesn't use water. Instead, it uses bags to wrap and seal up every deposit so there's no smell or mess. The reason I'd switch to the Laveo for a rental is that no matter how much it's explained, the composting toilet seems to confuse or intimidate renters.

Finding space to work

A possible expense for the DIY'er is having to rent workspace or storage space, especially if you have cold seasons like we do here in Vermont. In some residential neighborhoods, you may have a ban on the long-term parking of campers in your driveway or yard, so you might have to look around for space if your camper doesn't fit in your garage. When I had a project over the winter, I was able to rent a corner of a heated warehouse used to store cars for the season, and got a lot more done than if I had it parked in my yard.

Hiring professionals

Many people chose to hire a professional camper restorer or renovator to take on the entire fix-up job. As mentioned earlier, in these parts it costs $1,200 to $2,500 a foot to have a pro do a full tear-down and rebuild of a camper—that means a tiny 12-foot camper could cost $14,400 to $30,000 to be completed. A 20-foot camper would cost $24,000 to $50,000. Since I don't have that kind of cash laying around, I decided to do it myself and learn along the way. It took two years to complete what I thought would take a couple months. For someone who wants a pristine and accurately restored camper that has some cleverly hidden modern updates—along with some peace of mind—hiring an expert or two may be the route to choose if you have the means to do so. You still may save over the cost of buying a camper that has already been restored, depending on what kind of camper it is and what materials are used.

The point here is not that you have to buy a new toilet, rent a space, or hire a pro, but that each decision can cost money. These expenses can really add up fast, and need to be considered when you're thinking of buying and fixing up an old trailer.

13

MAKING MISTAKES

EVEN SO-CALLED 'HARMLESS' MISTAKES can be frustrating and time consuming. But for the record, the bad mistakes are worse.

When my 1972 Airstream Argosy 20 Zola was finished, I was so excited to finally able to take her camping. Dwayne and I took an anniversary trip to a state park, and a trip to Tennessee for a camper rally. I did a solo trip to the Midwest and back with her. I did a solo cross-country trip to Santa Bar-

At a rest stop looking over the Pacific ocean on Highway 1.

bara, California, up the coast to San Francisco and back across the country. All went smoothly with the exception that my solar panel mysteriously disappeared on my way back from California, somewhere between Wyoming and Vermont.

After all this tripping, the following two seasons I rented her out to several people both as an Airbnb and through Outdoorsy. On the day after a rental, I had her parked out in front of our house to give her a bath and a deep clean. When I went into the camper, I smelled something musty. It wasn't very strong; I thought it might be the new coir I had put in the composting toilet. I opened up the windows to let the breeze go through and freshen things up.

I went through my usual cleaning steps and then prepared to fill the water tank. I checked the current water level and was surprised that the last renters had used up the entire tank since they only

There was a huge issue hiding under this countertop for months before it made itself clear.

rented for three days/nights, but I figured *who am I to judge a renter's cleanliness or liquid intake?* Come to think of it, the previous couple of renters had used most of the tank up, too. Even with this strange coincidence, without a thought I filled up the tank. As usual, I continually checked the water level, and stopped filling it when it was near-full.

Then, again as I always did, I switched on the water pump and turned on the kitchen faucet to make sure everything was working properly. The water pump started humming and pumping, and water predictably came out of the faucet—and then stopped.

I checked the tank and water pump, and they were both fine. I turned off the pump and turned it back on again. It was running fine, but no water was coming out of the faucet. I was mystified. What's going on with this thing?

Then I saw it: the river of water gushing out from under the base cabinet, rushing across the floor in various directions. I turned off the pump, grabbed a roll of paper towels, and started frantically pulling off paper towel sheets and throwing them into the lake forming in my camper. After scrambling to sop up as much water as I could, I checked the main water lines and couldn't find anything wrong. I followed the path of the water and it led to the front door and the refrigerator areas. I slid the fridge out and felt the floor. I pushed down on it, and my heart dropped. Rot. #%@$%ing ROT in my renovated camper's underlayment! WTH? It took almost 50 years for the previous floor to rot, how could this have happened so quickly? *What have these renters done to my camper?*

I gingerly turned on the pump again to see if I could spot a leak. I finally looked behind the base cabinet and saw water flowing out of a broken part of hose just beyond my reach. I eventually got the hose out, and saw that it was shredded. This was evidence of a water line that had frozen and burst. Despite being pretty sure that I emptied all the water from the camper before winter, here was proof that I didn't. And it obviously had been leaking long before it burst.

I neglected to properly winterize my water pipes, which resulted in time-extensive costly fixes.

I'd like to draw your attention to the phrase I used in the last paragraph—I was "pretty sure" that I emptied all the water. I knew immediately what I did—or rather, what I didn't do. In my rush to get the camper prepped for winter the previous year, I decided Zola would be fine without having

Instead of setting my camper on fire, I pulled up the flooring to find that the underlayment under the fridge and by the door was rotten and moldy. Even though the subfloor seemed fine, I decided to replace that, too.

RV waterline antifreeze in the lines to protect against exactly what happened. The pipes and tank looked empty so I thought there would be no problem. Plus, I'd save a step in the spring if I didn't have to empty that pink antifreeze stuff out of my water lines, right?

Well, I was right about one thing. I did not in fact have to empty pink antifreeze stuff out of my water lines.

My first thought after this discovery and realization was not "OK, let's see what's going on and fix it!" It was *I should set this piece of sh*t on fire*. It took couple days to get a some band-aids to stick precariously to my battered ego, and I forced myself to go back to the camper and do some serious assessing. I took out the fridge and the chairs in the front. I pulled off the trim around the edge of the linoleum flooring. I accepted the fact that the underlayment was damaged, so I pulled up all of the linoleum and underlayment. I decided to pull up about a third of the subfloor as a precaution.

Zola has been partially dismantled and re-sealed. While she was empty, I decided to make a handful of changes, some of which I still have to get done. She'll get a new coat of interior paint in the spring. I'm adding a new $400 three-burner slide-in propane cooktop that I was happy to find for $60 on Facebook Marketplace. I have a new solar panel to install since I hadn't put one back on since that California trip. And, of course, the camper needs new plumbing.

Sweating the small stuff

Thankfully, most mistakes are a lot less soul-ripping. For example, I thought I found THE table for my little Airstream after I put it in and took it out of my Wayfair shopping cart over several months until it went on sale. I had measured and re-measured my diner-booth chairs and compared the specs of table to the specs of the chairs. Then I compared the specs of the new water tank I planned to put under part of the table, and according to all details, everything would fit perfectly. The table had a half-round drop leaf on one side—a bonus that made it more perfect.

The "perfect" table turned out to be a fail.

On the day it arrived, my camper was done enough so that I had room to assemble the table and put it in place. It was months before I would be camping or permanently installing the chairs and table, but I couldn't wait to see how all these exceptional, well-researched purchases looked and worked together. Sixteen screws and eight bolts later the table was put together. I flipped it over and moved it into place.

My newly assembled table—the table I'd measured and remeasured and was so confident in—didn't fit at all. It didn't fit around the water tank, and the chair seat was too wide to fit between

When I discovered that the inside wheel well pushed the outside wheel well too close to the tires, I installed spacers to solve the issue.

the legs of the table. To get on the chair required climbing up onto the chair, maneuvering legs under the table, and awkwardly dropping into the seat. Getting out was more complicated.

I was disappointed, but it wasn't traumatic or long-lived. The table found its way out of the camper, and now functions as my front-porch table after I epoxied it and put a hole in the middle for an umbrella. In the realm of mistakes, it was a fairly inexpensive and easy to fix—I just took it out of the camper.

My first patches were done with the wrong rivets and looked like crap, but at least they still don't leak.

There was the time I accidentally hammered my chisel through the roof of a camper when trying to remove a rivet. Go ahead, laugh… I did after the mortified anguish went away. I even laughed the second time I did it a year later. The result is that I learned how to patch holes in aluminum (and how to properly use a chisel). Months later after I'd made my first patches using interior rivets rather than buck rivets I learned that this was a no-no—I made them waterproof by coating the seam and rivets with Vulkem caulking to prevent leaks. Basically, I didn't know when I started this process that there were different kinds of rivets for different kinds of jobs.

I read. I stood and stared and tried to gain perspective on my situation. I found leaks and fixed them, then found more leaks and fixed them. I asked a lot of questions. I learned from people on Facebook, in forums, on YouTube. I learned where to look for rust and rot, and found it. I taught myself how to wire 110 and 12v. I got POR 15 in my hair and caulking and paint on nearly all of my clothes.

I watched videos about RV plumbing. I installed a solar panel and system. I learned how to cut aluminum and how to rivet three different ways (once I realized there were three different kinds of rivets I could use). Sometimes I got help—one brother welded on a new outrigger for me, and another brother helped me change the axle. Sometimes people who said they would help me were no-shows, and I figured out the solution myself. For example, I was promised help with reinstalling the original interior end cap because it required three people to install. Since I couldn't get help, I built a new endcap since I could install it by myself.

I installed insulation, built walls, and created a new layout. I fixed dents, waterproofed, primed, painted. I cut and installed a new bellypan. I added a cargo door. And on and on. Is it perfect? Absolutely not. But it was mine, and I had no regrets other than accidentally giving myself a third-degree burn with a hot Dremel blade. Don't do that.

When I couldn't go any further without an endcap in place and help was nowhere to be found, I switched gears and made a new endcap out of aluminum. I learned how by trial and error, forum photo albums, and instructional videos.

Back in the saddle

I wish I could tell you that I bravely picked myself up and dusted myself off, got back in the saddle, pulled myself up by my bootstraps, and all those other optimistic idioms. I wasn't feeling any of those things. I hate making mistakes, and the water pipe burst/Zola re-rebuild one triggered both depression and embarrassment. I know I am supposed to be telling you that everyone makes mistakes, and to find more idioms and proverbial phrases to inspire you to forge ahead, like life giving you lemons.

I finally told a friend about it.

My biggest mistake with the belly pan? Not asking for help. I learned fast that it's tough (shall we say, impossible?) for one person to hold up sheets of aluminum in place to attach to the frame, so I set up stabilizer jacks and pieces of wood to act as helping hands.

"That's a new chapter for your book!" she said excitedly, obviously oblivious to the pity party I wanted to hang out in. "That's so great!"

While I wasn't feeling the same level of excitement that she was feeling about it, I agreed. I set out writing this book wanting to be real about the entire process so that if you decide to delve into one of these crazy projects, you'd feel like you have a little more guidance than I did. And that means that I have to tell you about my mistakes—not just the little ones, but the big what-the-blank-have-I-done ones.

In short, mistakes are inevitable, especially if you are new to all of this like I was. Every single person who has taken on this kind of project has had to do it a first time.

14

RESOURCES

I AM SO GRATEFUL for all of the resources, companies, places, and people I've had the luck to learn from. I'm sharing some of my favorites that I hope you'll have the chance to experience, too. I'm also sharing a list of campgrounds that rent vintage and classic campers for you to stay in so you can give this travel trailer stuff a try. One I have been to on Route 66 is pictured above—Enchanted Trails RV Park & Trading Post in Albuquerque, NM.

BOOKS

The Illustrated Field Guide to Vintage Trailers
Bob Thompson and Carl Jameson, 2019

Normally I hesitate to call a book a 'must have', but *The Illustrated Field Guide to Vintage Trailers* by Bob Thompson and Carl Jameson is definitely an exception. Not only does it list pretty much every vintage travel trailer ever known, it also takes time to teach us about the historical styles of travel trailer (canned ham, breadloaf, etc.) and the pros and cons of each. Full of photos and drawings, brand and model history, identification hints, and other information, it's definitely a book you want to bring with you when scouting out an old camper or attending a vintage camper rally. It's not a book you read once and stow away. The only drawback is that it made me want to get a lot more campers. Like, every one. 320 pages.

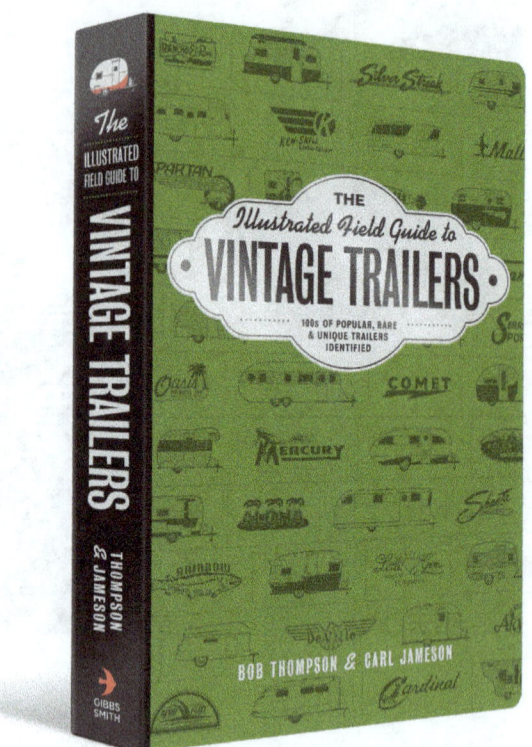

Photo courtesy of Bob Thompson and Carl Jameson

Camper Rehab: A Guide to Buying, Repairing, and Upgrading Your Travel Trailer
Chris Peterson, 2017

Camper Rehab covers both older and newer travel trailers, including a section that describes the benefits of different sizes and features. It also has a good how-to-buy section. It covers several aspects of camper fixer-upping, including painting, polishing, electrical systems, wheel and axle care, fixing door frames, understanding plumbing, and more. While it doesn't dive deep into any one part of rehab, it does have clear how-tos and gives newcomers an overview of the scope of work necessary to take care of many of the aspects of renovation and restoring. 224 pages.

All Things Camper Renovating: How to DIY your way through an RV renovation and transform an ugly camper into a stylish home on wheels
Sarah Lemp, 2020

Sarah's book is beautiful and cheerleaderly inspirational for those who are wondering what to do with the aesthetic element of their project, and includes some information on structural and systems. It's a super-fast read. The book includes the work of several other camper owners as well as her own, and I particularly like the before/after comparisons. It covers RVs of all ages, including brand new. Note: there is a lot of white paint in these projects! 228 pages.

Tin Can Homestead: The Art of Airstream Living
Natasha Lawyer and Brett Bashaw, 2018

Tin Can Homestead is a favorite book of many new old-Airstream owners, and I found it to be of interest to other camper owners, too. Natasha and Brett share the story of how they caught the tiny living bug while living and traveling in their 1978 Volkswagon bus. This sparked their interest in later buying and living in a vintage Airstream. It has beautiful photos and illustrations, and includes some how-to. It's important to keep in mind that they designed their Airstream to be stationary, so the build did not have to take road travel into account. 216 pages.

Glamping with Maryjane
Maryjane Butters, 2012

While there is a savvy section dedicated to scoping out and buying a camper, *Glamping with MaryJane* is primarily a perspective on and practical guide for decorating, camping, and traveling in glamper-luxury. It's full of inspiring photos and projects, as well as advice on safety, what to pack, and suggestions on where to go. 224 pages.

Vintage Camper Trailers
Paul & Caroline Lacitinola, 2016

If the name of this book sounds familiar, it's because this book is written by the founders of *Vintage Camper Trailers Magazine*. If you're looking for inspiration and ideas, this is a great start. Full of photos, it also includes stories about the people whose campers are featured. 200 pages.

Photo courtesy of Paul & Caroline Lacitinola

Vintage Trailer Style: Buying, Restoring, Decorating & Styling the Small Place of Your Dreams
Lisa Mora, 2014

Vintage Trailer Style is full of beautiful photos and the basics of choosing and designing a camper that suits the reader's style. It covers finding a camper to choosing a color and personality theme, to traveling and joining communities that have the same interests. *Vintage Trailer Style* is difficult to find, so when you find a copy, keep it close so you can flip through when you need an inspirational boost. Lisa is the founder of *Vintage Caravan Magazine*, which is now *Vintage Trailer Magazine*. 144 pages.

Restoring a Dream: My Journey Restoring a Vintage Airstream
Tim Shephard, 2013

Restoring a Dream was one of the first books I purchased when I got interested in vintage Airstreams. This book by the founder of theVAP podcast, where I first heard of the terms 'polished turd' and 'aluminum tent'. The book includes his personal story with buying and restoring his vintage Airstream, along with a wide array of practical information, from seam sealing to torsion axles. It's a good read even if you're not into Airstreams. 298 pages.

MAGAZINES

Vintage Trailer Magazine, which started out as *Vintage Caravan Magazine* in 2011. [vintagetrailermagazine.com]

Vintage Camper Trailers Magazine not only has a print publication, it also hosts several vintage camper rallies and the Vintage Camper Bootcamp, a four-day camper renovation intensive held every spring in California. *Vintage Camper Trailers Magazine* has an extensive classifieds section. [classifieds.vintagecampertrailers.com]

Trailer Life, in publication since 1941, generally covers current campers, but also has coverage of vintage trailer rallies, renovations, and lifestyles. [www.trailerlife.com]

MATERIALS & SUPPLIES

Vintage Trailer Supply

VTS is a hugely popular store, and has a super-wide inventory selection of vintage and reproduction parts including its own products. Things I've purchased: Those fuzzy things that go in the slot on the screen to keep bugs out, reproduction light fixtures, o-rings, rivets, marker lights, molding, trim, caulk, and more. The company was originally based in Montpelier, Vermont, and moved its home base to Santa Fe, New Mexico not long ago.

[vintagetrailersupply.com]

Airparts Inc.

Airparts is my favorite resource for aluminum and pretty much anything to do with aluminum, and will ship anywhere in the U.S. It is the company that I've turned to for rolls of belly-pan aluminum, clecos, and buck rivets. They are a family owned and run business based in Kansas, and they are always a pleasure to purchase from. [airpartsinc.com]

Hemet Valley RV Siding and Storage
[hemetvalleyrv.net]
I haven't purchased from Hemet, so I can't share a personal experience with them. I feel I should mention them, though, since they come up in conversation nearly every time someone has a need for the patterned aluminum siding that many vintage and classic campers use.

INSPIRATION & INFORMATION

Miller Garage TV
[youtube.com/c/MillerGarage]

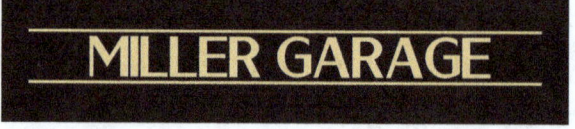

I stumbled on the Miller Garage YouTube channel 2018 video, "Airstream Shell Lift Part 1 — We Almost Died // 1976 Renovation" in early 2020. I was originally looking for information regarding lifting an Airstream off of its frame in order to replace its subfloor. My curiosity piqued at the 'almost died' part because, as you might guess, I didn't want to die putting in a subfloor. I've been watching Miller Garage videos ever since. Miller Garage is now a full-time professional renovator based in Texas.

Mortons on the Move
[mortonsonthemove.com]
I couldn't have put together my electrical system without the Morton's assistance. They live and travel full-time in their RV, and share their knowledge and experiences through YouTube videos and blog posts that I've bookmarked and referred to over and over. They are not vintage camper owners, but much of their information can be applied to those of us without a newish travel trailer. I haven't found another resource that can match Tom Morton's instructions and explanations through technical details. Plus, the videos often have an accompanying blog post that I can refer to easier than trying to find something in a video again.

Long Long Honeymoon

[longlonghoneymoon.com]

The Michaels became Airstreamers on their wedding honeymoon, and pretty much have kept honeymooning since. Their series cover all kinds of topics about travel and upkeep, including being kicked out of a campground for having a travel trailer that was "too old," to buying gifts for camperaholics, to how to deal with black tank issues and more. Their YouTube video "How To Buy an Airstream Travel Trailer" features veteran restorer Tim Heintz of Heintz Designs and is a good primer in buying new and vintage. [longlonghoneymoon.com/category/vintage/ or youtu.be/06Euf0ICHOQ]

RENTING VINTAGE CAMPERS

Airbnb

Airbnb lists several vintage campers for rent at the owner's property. You can go through Airbnb's the reservation search and browse through all of the listings in the area you want to stay in. I've found it quicker to search through Google by typing *airbnb.com: vintage camper destination*, where 'destination' is where you want to go, like *vermont* or *memphis*. I've also used *airbnb.com: glamper destination*, i.e. *airbnb.com: glamper smoky mountain*. [airbnb.com]

Outdoorsy

Similar to Airbnb, Outdoorsy is a service for owners of campers so that they can rent to the public. The trailer listing should include whether or not you can tow it yourself, how far you can tow, how long you can use it, and whether the owners insist that they handle towing to, setting up, and towing back from your destination. I have rented both ways, since those new to using a travel trailer usually prefer not to tow someone else's camper as their first experience. You can search for a camper near your destination from the home page. [outdoorsy.com]

CAMPGROUNDS RENTING VINTAGE CAMPERS

Some of the following campsites offer space for you to bring your own camper, some are a collection of their own camper accommodations.

Kate's Lazy Desert, Landers, CA [lazymeadow.com/lazy-desert-ca]
Founded by Kate Pierson of the B-52's and her wife, artist Monica Nation. And if that's not cool enough, it features six vintage Airstreams in the Mohave desert renovated by different area artists.

The Shady Dell, Bisbee, AZ [theshadydell.com]
The Shady Dell, located about an hour and half Southeast of Tucson, has over a dozen vintage campers for rent from the 1940s and 1950s.

Hotel Luna Mystica, Taos, NM [hotellunamystica.com]
Twenty classic and vintage campers can be rented at Hotel Luna Mystica, or you can bring your own. One of their travel trailers is a 1957 Spartan Imperial Mansion that has eight bunk beds and a queen bed so you can bring the whole family and then some.

The Vintages Trailer Resort, Dayton, OR [the-vintages.com]
The Vintages has 35 travel trailers to rent from the 40s, 50s, 60s, 70s, 90s, and 2000s, including some Neutrons, a retro-inspired travel trailer built by Flyte Camp in Bend, OR.

JuneBug Retro Resort, Weaverville, NC [junebugretroresort.com]
Just minutes from Asheville, JuneBug features 10 travel trailers for rent, including a couple of Spartanettes, a couple of Trotwoods, and more.

El Cosmico, Marfa, TX [elcosmico.com]
About an hour north of the Mexican border in the Chihuahuan Desert, El Cosmico has a selection of small, medium, large, and extra-large vintage campers for rent in the artistic enclave of Marfa.

BEFORE YOU BUY A VINTAGE CAMPER

Sou'wester Historic Lodge and Vintage Travel Trailer Resort, Seaview, WA [souwesterlodge.com]
The Sou'wester has a fleet of over 30 vintage travel trailers from the 1950s and 1960s.

El Pais Motel, Tucson, AZ [elpaismotel.com]
As part of their tiny-space accommodation offerings, El Pais has two vintage Airstreams for rent.

Waypoint Ventura, Ventura, CA [waypointventura.com]
Waypoint has 20 vintage and classic campers for rent at its campground, 10 of which are restored, and the other ten have been renovated with what they refer to as "modern luxury."

The Trailer Pond, Paso Robles, CA [thetrailerpond]
Tucked into the Alta Colina Vineyard around a private pond, The Trailer Pond has five glamped up travel trailers from the 1950s and 1960s.

Desert Sands Trailer Park, Borrego Springs, CA [desertsandsrvpark.net]
Desert Sands has a handful of vintage and classic travel trailers for rent in its fleet, tucked in the middle of the Anza-Borrego State Park, the largest in California.

Pinecrest Retreat, Julian, CA [pinecrestretreat.squarespace.com]
Pinecrest has 1950s to 1970s vintage and classic travel trailers for rent in its campground.

Tiger Drive-in, Tiger, GA [tigerdrivein.com]
A drive-in theatre with vintage campers to rent! What are you waiting for?

Enchanted Trails RV Park & Trading Post, Albuquerque, NM [enchantedtrails.com]
Besides larger family sized travel trailers for rent, Enchanted Trails has a teeny 1956 teardrop trailer, a weensie 1963 Winnebago, and wee 1954 VaKaShunette to choose from. The Winnebago and VaKaShunette are shown in the photo at the beginning of this chapter.

CRYSTAL MCCULLOUGH

Zack at the end of the double rainbow.

GLOSSARY

Battery: The center of the power system in a camper. It stores power for use by appliances and devices when you're not plugged in.

Black water: The stuff that you flush out of your toilet.

Blue boy: A cart used to haul black and gray water to a dumping area.

Boondocking: Camping without being plugged in or hooked up to a water source or sewer connection.

Bumper pull: A camper that is pulled by a hitch attached under the rear bumper.

Bunkhouse: A camper that includes two or more bunkbeds to increase sleeping areas.

Cassette toilet: A toilet that has a removeable black tank (the cassette) that you empty into a dump station or honey wagon.

GLOSSARY

Converter: Turns AC power into DC power to charge your battery and to use 12-volt devices.

Coupler: The part of a trailer's tongue that clamps down on the hitch ball for towing.

Curb weight: The weight of a camper when it's empty.

Curbside or curb side: The side of the camper that faces the road's curb as you tow it. The door is on the curb side.

Dry camping: See *boondocking*

Dry weight: See *curb weight*

Dually: A truck that has four wheels/tires on the rear axle; two on each side.

Dump station: A facility where you can empty out your black and gray tanks, Blue Boy, or cassette from your cassette toilet.

Equalizer hitch: A hitch that distributes the weight being held up by your hitch and rear tow-vehicle axle to your rear and front axle. This makes driving and towing safer.

Fifth wheel (or 5th wheel): A camper that is designed to attach to a special hitch in the bed of a truck. Part of the camper hangs over the back of the tow vehicle.

Fresh water tank: The storage tank for your clean water.

Full hookup: When you attach to power, water, and sewer at a campsite. Sometimes a full hookup will include cable television.

Full-timer: Person who lives and/or travels in their travel trailer or motorhome full time.

Gaucho: A sofa that folds or pulls out to be a bed. The cushions of the gaucho rearrange to become the mattress.

Gray water: This is all wastewater that isn't what you flush, i.e., water from your shower and sink.

Hitch weight/tongue weight: This is the amount of weight that your trailer tongue puts on the hitch.

Holding tanks: The tanks that hold your fresh water, gray water, and black water.

Honey wagon: A truck that pumps sewage and gray water out of the camper's holding tanks when there are no dump stations or sewer hookups available.

Hookups (also see *full hookups*): What your camper hooks up to when parked, such as power, water, and sewer.

Inverter: An inverter converts power from your battery into AC power when you aren't hooked up to shore power.

Leveling jacks: Legs that are attached to the underside of a camper that are lowered to the ground to level out the camper both backward and forward, and from side to side. They are designed to hold weight.

LP gas: LP stands for 'liquid propane', and is often the fuel for camper stoves, hot water heaters, and furnaces. It is carried in tanks that are often placed on the trailer tongue.

GLOSSARY

Motorhome: A camper that has the living area and motorized propulsion in the same vehicle rather than a separate trailer and tow vehicle.

Part-timers: People who spend part of the year living in their camper.

Pull-through: A campground site that allows you to drive into and out of it without having to back up.

RV: Abbreviation for 'recreational vehicle'.

Self-contained: A camper that has all the elements inside it to be able to stay in it without having to use external sources. For example, if the camper has a shower, there's no need to use a campground shower. If the camper doesn't have a refrigerator, then you might need to go buy food every day or have a cooler rigged up to power in your tow vehicle.

Shore power: Power that you access when you are parked. Your camper plugs into shore power.

Snowbird: A person who travels to a warmer climate in the colder months of the year.

Stability jacks: Jacks used to stabilize a camper so it doesn't rock, but not to lift a camper (see *leveling jacks*).

Street side: The side of your travel trailer that faces the road when you are parked on the side of the road. The opposite side is the curb side.

Sway bars (also *sway control*): Usually installed in conjunction with weight distribution, they help to keep the towed trailer from wobbling back and forth behind the tow vehicle.

Toy hauler: A camper that combines living/sleeping space with a space in which to tow a motorcycle, four-wheeler, or other recreational vehicle.

Tow rating: The amount of weight the manufacturer has determined is safe to pull with your tow vehicle.

Travel Trailer: A camper with an A-shaped hitch that you pull with a tow vehicle.

Truck camper: A camper attached to a truck frame that slides into the bed of the truck.

TV: Abbreviation for 'tow vehicle'.

A vintage truck-camper seen at the Pismo rally.

Two- and three-way refrigerators: A three-way RV refrigerator can run on AC (shore) and DC (battery) power, as well as propane. A two-way runs off of two of the three.

Weight distribution hitch: see *Equalizer hitch*

Wheel chocks: Wedges made from plastic or other material that is placed in front of and/or in back of tires to keep a vehicle or trailer from rolling.

Workamping: Also called *work camping*, it's when you travel to a place in order to work there in exchange for camping space and hookups, and possibly an income. Many people use workamping gigs to pay for their travels. See workamper.com to see what kinds of opportunities available, and join if you want specific information that members get access to.

GLOSSARY

Another fun day of frame repair.

AUTHOR'S STORY

I'M CRYSTAL WATERS McCULLOUGH, and for the record, I didn't crop my dog's nose out of our co-selfie, he did. In this picture, I'm in one of my happiest places—with a 1970s camper in progress (Zack), and a dog (Dawkins). I tried to get my other dog Lexie in the picture, but she was off smelling or chasing something very, very important. I'm married to Dwayne, the best husband in the world because he indulges my passion of rescuing old campers and writing books about them. We live in Vermont with our cat Gilly, who rules over us all. I do a lot of writing and editing, and have been doing both professionally since the late 1980s. Besides writing, editing, and campering, I do several other things including designing and drawing retro wallpaper that is inspired by those in old campers.

This is my ninth book as an author or co-author, and the first about buying an old camper.

How this camper stuff became more than just camper stuff

I am not alone in having a travel trailer change my life. This is how they have changed mine.

A few years ago, I experienced of a number of losses that happened in quick succession. What I didn't know yet is that besides grieving, I was suffering from depression, PTSD, anxiety, and OCD (the real kind, not the "I'm SO..." kind), and had been since I was a kid. I thought I was just a quirky kid that grew up into a quirky adult. In any case, this series of losses triggered all of these conditions. My self-confidence and self-worth were not showing up for duty, and all of this stuff was augmented by a premenopausal and menopausal hormonal roller coaster. I was confused. *What is going on with me? I'm a successful editor! I've written books! I have great references! I am smiling! See me smiling??*

My eighth book, A Quick-Read Guide to Organizing a 5K, is available on Amazon and Barnes & Noble.

Around the same time, my newish obsessiveness with getting a camper was developing some unhealthy practices, too. For example, I'd find myself spending hours searching every craigslist across the country, calculating what I could and should spend and going back and forth about what I wanted and putting random camper things in my Amazon shopping cart rather than taking care of things based in reality. I was using the camper search to distract from the pain. It helped some, but not enough.

I hit a bottom with OCD that was exacerbated by the suicide of a dear friend in early 2017. I started feeling like I did on the way to my alcoholic bottom 20 years prior. Before I got sober, on the outside, things looked neat and tidy. But on the inside, it was pretty much sh*t. *See me smiling? See?!?* The very short version of what happened next: At my next annual physical, I talked to my doctor, who suggested therapy. I'd done that several times, but hadn't since I lived in San Francisco when I went to couples therapy by myself. Thankfully, this time around I was able to become a regular patient with an amazing psychiatrist. And I'm not just saying that about her because she's reading this. I continue to work with her now.

Not everything was horrible during that time frame. I started and ended a race-timing business, and wrote a book about directing 5K running races (I've since written a second edition). In the late summer of 2016, I was accepted into the Yale Publishing Course Leadership Strategies in Book Publishing certificate program. For lack of a better way to describe it, it was f'ing awesome. It had been nearly 20 years since studying Business Press Publishing at NYU, and it was inspiring to be among all of these professionals. I came out of the course determined to start my own publishing imprint. I took on projects with potential authors, and helped develop some amazing book ideas. But the imprint suffered with all the above stuff hanging overhead, and it didn't grow a fraction as successfully and quickly as I'd projected. I was doing the work but my heart wasn't in it. I was, however, making progress in therapy, which in turn helped me start to make progress again in my work.

Um, yeah... but weren't we talking about campers?

Why am I telling you this personal stuff, and how in the world does any of this correlate to buying old campers? Working on my first classic camper represented what I'd been going through for the previous few years. I know that to many people, Zola is just an old camper that I bought from a guy in Missouri that I've fixed up. To me, she's a representative of my own examination, healing, and rebuilding. She gave me permission to look inside the walls, to acknowledge and tear out the rot and ruin, and forced me to put her back together whether I knew how or not. I made a space I could

AUTHOR'S STORY

Bad hair days, too, shall pass.

travel in that was safe, and was able to lift up my head and be accountable, face what was wrong, and commit to something a day at a time.

Searching for just the right camper and searching for answers in therapy are both really hard work. Both can be emotional, stressful, exciting, and rewarding. The process of fixing up a camper and fixing up a life are both slower than I want or expect. I was raised to believe that if you don't think or talk about things, then they didn't happen. I could have just painted over the rot and mouse corpses and gone camping like many purchasers of old campers do, but I'd still know that it/they were there. No matter how much I shoved thoughts and memories away, they were still there, and things still happened even if I didn't want them to have happened. Dead mice are there even if you pretend they aren't. The only way for me to be sane and happy is to face things head-on—in the camper, that could mean literally removing mice and assessing all of the issues and problems in front of me; in life that has meant building a trusting relationship with a therapist and working on issues that have happened and as they come up. Doing them at the same time has given me perspective and strength I had been missing for a long time.

Wait a minute… are you saying that I have to be depressed to buy an old camper?

No. You can, in fact, be mentally and emotionally stable and still shop for and buy an old camper. If you need some help someday, I encourage you to ask for it. I've listed some resources below.

Resources for information and help for a few of the non-camper parts of life

- If you are in a crisis situation, call 911 or go to the nearest emergency room.

- The National Institute of Mental Health (NIMH): nimh.nih.gov
Information on several classifications of mental illness and what kind of treatment is available.

- National Suicide Prevention Lifeline: suicidepreventionlifeline.org
800-273-TALK (800-273-8255)

- Finding a therapist: psychologytoday.com/us/therapists

- What is OCD?
psychiatry.org/patients-families/ocd/what-is-obsessive-compulsive-disorder

- Alcoholics Anonymous—aa.org

AUTHOR'S STORY

Hi, Dad.

ERRATA, ET CETERA

Photo credits

All photos are by the author unless marked otherwise. Those images marked AS are licensed for use from Adobe Stock. [stock.adobe.com]

Contact and/or follow the author

Email: crystal@tinandrivet.com
Web: www.tinandrivet.com
Instagram: @tinandrivet
Facebook: @zolasdiary
Patreon: patreon.com/tinandrivet

Other neato things made by the author

Wallpaper and fabric designs: spoonflower.com/profiles/ernts
Statement knits: etsy.com/shop/ernts

Errata

I wish I were perfect, but, alas, am not so much. If you find a typo or factual inaccuracy, please send corrections and suggestions to me at crystal@tinandrivet.com. Thank you!

www.ingramcontent.com/pod-product-compliance
Lightning Source LLC
Chambersburg PA
CBHW081410080526
44589CB00016B/2521